SUPERVISION:

Developing and Directing People on Mission

Doran C. McCarty

D1262399

Published by
SEMINARY EXTENSION
of the Southern Baptist Seminaries
901 Commerce St., Suite 500
Nashville, Tennessee 37203-3631

CONTENTS

DEDICATION

This book is affectionately dedicated
to two long-time friends:

FRED PRYOR

and

ELWYN HAYS

FOREWORD

by Jerry Rankin

People involved in missions are usually highly motivated due to a sense of divine call and personal relationship to God. While this often strengthens a tendency toward independence and individualism, it is evident that missionaries must relate to one another appropriately if they are to be effective. This is especially true where one is a part of a team of ministers in a common location or assignment with others.

For the relationship among missionaries to have a synergistic effect, there must be mutual respect, accountability to one another, and also accountability to the organization or sponsoring body. This is necessary to assure that individual efforts are consistent with the purpose of the sponsoring organization and that the results of a person's ministry conform to the expectations and objectives of the assignment.

Usually "supervision" is thought of in terms of the submission of one individual or group to the authority of another. However, supervision is effective only when it is implemented within a team concept. It is more than knowing the skills of administration, but it also involves the attitudes and understanding of the person being supervised.

It must never be forgotten that supervision is for the benefit and advantage of the one being supervised, not simply for the organization. It allows the organization, the local mission, institution, or ministry to be an enabler and an equipper by providing practical, hands-on training, guidance, and encouragement on a continuing basis.

Many missionaries have multi-levels of responsibility and multi-directional accountability. For example, one may relate to the sponsoring body, to a local organization, to the local church, to colleagues, supervisors, boards, etc. This can create a great deal of anxiety and frustration if there are no clear lines of communication and guidance.

Supervision must be a relationship that transcends the organizational structure. It should always be seen in terms of the development of a person and one's potential rather than simply an effort to maximize results. It can work only where there is a mutual commitment to each other and to the ministry or task.

Jerry Rankin, President
The Foreign Mission Board, SBC

FOREWORD

by Larry Lewis

A predecessor of mine once had a plaque on his desk that said, "People Count." What was true then is still true today. The Home Mission Board is concerned about people. Developing support systems so missions personnel might grow personally and be productive is the central focus of our investment in supervision training. The Home Mission Board is concerned that our missionaries be given every opportunity to succeed in their ministry, and we believe quality supervision is the best way to achieve that result.

As an agency, we must be good stewards of people resources. Through supervision training, the framework is put in place for caring for people and being accountable for the work of ministry. I hope we will apply the principles of this book to the practice of ministry.

Larry Lewis, President
The Home Mission Board, SBC

PREFACE

A new awareness of the importance of working together has developed in the past three decades. The importance of leadership, total quality management, and the team approach have influenced business. A renewed emphasis on the priesthood of the believer has stimulated lay ministry among Southern Baptists. These factors have stimulated mission agencies to examine how supervision could be done within the context of the Free Church tradition.

When I was a professor of Christian theology and philosophy at Midwestern Baptist Theological Seminary, Kansas City, Missouri, the faculty gave me the additional assignment of directing student field supervision. That assignment began my interest in supervision. I was fortunate to receive training from the Boston Theological Institute/Notre Dame New Field Education Directors' Institute and to become a fellow in the Case Study Institute. I have also been fortunate to work with the Association of Theological Field Education and the Southern Baptist Fellowship of In-Service Guidance Directors.

My interest in mission supervision began when Paul Adkins of the Home Mission Board asked me to spend a sabbatical leave doing research with the Christian social ministries department of the Home Mission Board, examining their processes of supervision and continuing education. During the intervening years, I have been working with schools, the supervision system of the Home Mission Board, and other agencies on supervision.

The Home Mission Board has set up a supervision training system for persons whom it appoints, assigns, and others (for example mission volunteers). Working with Southern Baptist state conventions, the Board has trained people from every state in the country. Bob Mills, director of the Mission Service Corps department, has done an excellent job of providing a team of seminar leaders to lead these training events.

The first book to come from these activities was *The Supervision of Ministry Students.* It was revised as *Supervising Ministry Students.* This work also produced *The Supervision of Mission Personnel.* This volume, *SUPERVISION: Developing and Directing People on Mission,* revises the previous book, providing responses to many issues that people have raised during supervision training seminars.

There are several people whom I should thank for their help in making this book possible. The first is Bob Mills. Few people have affected missions in the United States the way Bob Mills has done with his leadership with Mission Service Corps persons and developing the supervision training system. I want to thank all the supervision seminar participants who have made suggestions addressed in this book. I thank Glenn Prescott for his help in providing foreign mission perspectives. Thanks to Seminary Extension for giving me the opportunity to write this book. I thank the Home and Foreign Mission Boards that provided funds for this book. I thank the cadre of supervision trainers who made suggestions for the book. George Knight, Lesley Vance, and Kay Churchwell of Seminary Extension helped by providing editorial service for this publication.

Doran C. McCarty

CHAPTER 1

A BIBLICAL PERSPECTIVE

The Bible presents many examples of supervision but there is no one pattern. This reinforces my theory that there is no one "righteous" style, but there is the need to adapt styles to the situations.

BIBLICAL EXAMPLES

Each of the following biblical examples presents people who had supervisory responsibility. While there are many others I could include, these provide clear examples. I do not imply that there is one pattern here, nor that they all were perfect nor that their supervisory situations were the same as yours and mine.

Moses. Jethro, Moses' father-in-law, chided him because Moses was trying to do everything himself. [1] Jethro told Moses to teach people the rules and then appoint trustworthy people to be the "supervisors." Jethro recognized that the supervisory span was beyond Moses' ability to serve. Moses divided the people up by groups with "supervisors" who were responsible to him.

Elijah and Elisha. Elijah was a great prophet in the Old Testament. Jesus' experience with Moses and Elijah indicated the importance of Elijah. [2] Elijah was alone when he challenged

---

[1] Exodus 18:17.

[2] Matthew 17:3.

1

the Baalites at Mt. Carmel [3] but later chose Elisha to work with him. [4] We know little of the relationship of Elijah and Elisha. Apparently, like prophets at the time, Elijah had bands of prophets related to him in Bethel, Jericho and Jordan. We know the dramatic story of Elijah being taken from Elisha and Elisha crying, "My father, my father." [5]

Elisha had asked for a double portion of Elijah's "spirit" to be placed upon him when Elijah left. We can easily assume that Elisha had seen the great work (tasks) of Elijah but also had developed a close personal relationship that caused him to cry "My father, my father." I deduce from these events that the relationship was both task and personhood.

Eli and Samuel. Samuel's mother, Hannah, dedicated her son to the Lord and left him with the priest, Eli, to rear. Samuel served the Lord under Eli [6] and Eli directed Samuel through his call from the Lord. [7] While Eli served for forty years, probably no Hebrew leader between Moses and David was as powerful as Samuel. Since Eli's sons turned out badly, it appears that Eli turned his attention to the development of Samuel as his successor.

Jesus and the disciples. Jesus gave His greatest attention to His disciples. He began His ministry by recruiting them. He prepared them for the time when He would not be with them any longer. Jesus found this to be an arduous task because His disciples seemed to have their own agenda.

He taught them to pray. [8] Jesus was concerned about the disciples knowing how to pray though they knew about the prayers of the Pharisees and John the Baptist's disciples.

---

[3] 1 Kings 18.

[4] 1 Kings 19:19f.

[5] 2 Kings 2:12.

[6] 1 Samuel 2:18.

[7] 1 Samuel 3.

[8] Matthew 6:5-13.

He sent them out on a preaching mission. [9]   These were excellent examples of a supervisor helping others work and learn.   He gave them instructions about the message and the logistics.   When they returned, He evaluated the results and affirmed them and then gave them insights about what they would face in the future.

Paul and Timothy and others. Paul was a supervisor. We know of his relationships with Barnabas, Luke, Timothy, Titus, Onesimus and Aquila and Priscilla.   They were not only comrades in the faith but also benefitted from Paul being their supervisor.   Each brought his or her gifts.   They remained distinctive individuals rather than becoming clones of Paul. Sometimes Paul worked with them in close proximity (even sharing a jail cell) and other times he was their supervisor at a distance and had to depend upon writing letters.

SUPERVISION
AS A THEOLOGICAL ENTERPRISE

A supervisor in a Christian community is not theologically neutral.   The supervisor engages in such theological issues as creation, sanctification, discipleship, faith, hope, love, blessing, revealing, investing, showing grace and spirituality. [10]

The supervisor in a Christian community is developing a Kingdom person rather than training someone to be the administrator of an organization.   Whatever the supervisor does, there is an extra theological dimension.   Forgiveness is part of the Christian message just as effectiveness is part of an organization's work.   An organization may operate on the guidelines set out in a policy manual (law), but Christianity was founded on grace.

---

[9] Luke, chapters 9 and 10.

[10] For more on these subjects see my book, *The Inner Heart of Ministry* (Nashville: Broadman Press, 1985).

SUPERVISION AS MINISTRY

Pastors minister to people in their congregations, but when some become ministers it seems we do not think that we need to minister to them anymore. Ministers need ministry. They are still humans. They still are responsible to God.

Supervision is ministry. It is a ministry comparable to hospital ministry, counseling ministry, teaching ministry and evangelistic ministry. Good supervision can strengthen the Christian life and ministry of the missionary. Good supervision means that the missionary is not an errand runner but the extension of your own ministry.

Some businesses say that their employees are their most important resource. Missionaries are the most important resources of mission systems. They provide the ministry, presence and work of the mission system. If missionaries burn out or get "used up," the whole mission system suffers not only the loss of a missionary and the failure to achieve goals but the loss of integrity because of the mission system's insensitivity to missionaries' needs as persons.

The mission system gives a supervisor persons to work with whether the title is executive, director, supervisor or manager. The supervisor should ask: "What is the object of my ministry of supervision?" "Is the object a program or a person?" Every supervisor is either program-oriented or person-oriented. If the supervisor's central focus is on the program, the supervisor diminishes the personhood of the missionary. The supervisor's focus needs to be on the missionary who has a task to do.

Ministry means being sensitive to God and persons. Good ministry, therefore, means that supervisors will not try to manipulate and use God or persons. They will fulfill God's purpose in the Kingdom of God and care for the needs of persons. Ministry is about the Kingdom of God above all ("Seek ye first the Kingdom of God . . ." [11]). This raises the supervisor above dealing only with self-serving causes and using people to achieve self-serving ends.

---

[11] Matthew 6:33.

Every person has needs of the inner life — his or her spirituality. Busyness should not blind the supervisor to the inner heart of ministry. Spirituality is like the supply of manna in the wilderness; it must be renewed daily. The supervisor has a heart as well as a task, and the heart includes helping the mentor and supervisee develop as spiritual creatures.

CHAPTER 2

WHAT IS SUPERVISION?

This book is about how you can be a supervisor by developing mission personnel (appointed or voluntary) and directing mission work. Throughout the book there will be emphases on personhood and tasks. I make these emphases from the conviction that people are important and mission work needs to be done.

People are important! We have heard slogans about people being our greatest asset. It is true. Ministry is about people, and the people who do mission work deserve being the objects of ministry. As Jesus ministered to His disciples, we need to minister to those who minister. People need to grow as long as they live. Our job is to help that to happen. Mission people hurt, and they need healing from those who minister to them. When we invest in mission workers, we enhance mission work not only for the moment but for the whole term of their service to the Kingdom of God.

Mission work is important! We dare not forget that Jesus preached "The Kingdom of God" and we are to follow Him in this work. We always have limited resources. We work together as a community of faith. These demand that supervisors provide supervisorship to get tasks done.

Personhood and tasks are the two poles around which the material in this book will move. Often the emphasis upon personhood will be apparent because we have been influenced by a task-oriented society that loses sight of taking care of the people in the system. I have read thousands of reports from supervisors, and 98 percent are task-oriented. I am sure that if

6

I asked the persons who filled out these reports that they would tell me that they care about people and believe in a person-centered ministry. Underneath, most are task-oriented.

My purpose in this book is to help people in places of mission supervision responsibility understand how to enrich the lives of the people who work with them and to work with them by building a support system to get the mission work done. Many people in positions of mission supervision are doing these things but could do them better. Some do well sometimes but don't understand the principles that work for them so they can apply them to other situations.

NOMENCLATURE

Several years ago Gerald Palmer, at that time vice president of the Home Mission Board, asked me if there wasn't another word we could use other than supervision. I seldom hold a supervision seminar but what participants ask the same question. What term can we use to replace the word "supervision?" Some have suggested the word "coach." Others have suggested "mentor." Usually there are objections to these words. Let us look at the positive and negative contributions of these words for our task.

Supervisor

My definition of supervision is, "The development of a support systems for the enrichment of personhood and to assist in the performance of tasks."[1] As long as everyone thought of that definition when they heard the word "supervision," I am sure that we could use the word without hesitancy. However, the image many have of a supervisor is different than my definition. Many think of a supervisor as an ogre out of one of Dickens' tales. Others have flash backs of their basic training

---

[1] Doran C. McCarty, *Supervising Ministry Students* (Atlanta: Home Mission Board, SBC, 1978), p. 9.

sergeant in the military. Often I've heard, "You can't supervise Baptist preachers."

Commentary on the definition of supervision will help communicate what I mean by supervision. First, supervision is developmental. It goes through steps from one phase to another. As relationships and systems change, supervision develops.

Supervision is support. I would like to substitute the word "support" for "supervision." However, the word "support" brings its own set of baggage that is unclear. People often interpret support as only meaning providing financial resources. Nevertheless, supervision is a support system that strengthens the supervisee so that he or she may grow and get the task done. Support does not imply a frozen, saccharine-like, perpetual smile. Confrontation is one of the ways that we support people. David Augsburger wrote a book, *Caring Enough to Confront.*

Supervision is always a part of a system. Supervisors are not "Lone Rangers." As related to missions, supervisors are part of a missions system. There doesn't have to be anything vulgar or mysterious about systems. Systems are like gears in cars. Without gears in the transmission meshing, the car will go nowhere. When gears don't mesh, they make a lot of noise and heat. (Remember the sound when you turn the starter when the car is already running?) Systems work for people when people want them to work. Gears with too much slack will not work properly, allowing the car to "slip out of gear." Gears with no tolerance will probably not mesh, and, if they do, they will overheat. Systems in supervision need people who can mesh, but it takes some tolerance too.

Supervision functions to enrich personhood. Christian discipline, learning and self-examination are a few ways to enrich personhood. We are called to help people become better than they are and what God wants them to be. Redemption itself is the enrichment of personhood. As ministers we are doing what Virginia Satyr describes in the title of her book: *Peoplemaking.* The Christian gospel is about the business of peoplemaking, not buildings, nor agencies, nor books. These are only helps in peoplemaking.

Supervision assists in the performance of tasks. Camelot is not here so there is work yet to do. Supervision helps set goals, divide responsibilities, develop procedures and evaluate results.

Supervision is both enriching personhood and assisting in the performance of tasks. If either is left out, it is not supervision. Supervision keeps both in a creative tension. If we only deal with personhood, we are therapists, not supervisors. If a supervisee needs therapy, we should refer to a therapist even if we are qualified to do therapy because, if we do the therapy, we confuse and weaken our supervisory role.

If we deal with only tasks, we are no longer supervisors but administrators. While they are arbitrary definitions, I suggest that we supervise people and administrate programs.

Personhood and tasks are complementary, not irreconcilable opposites. I am convinced that the supervisor who takes care of personhood needs will find a supervisee wanting to get the tasks done. Also when the supervisor helps the supervisee get tasks done, the supervisee's personhood will be enriched.

We are still left with the wrong impression that many have of supervision being an over/under relationship that they believe is unchristian. Many have experienced supervision that is different than I have described. Also many have experienced bad supervision and don't want anything to do with it.

Mentor

Laurent Daloz opens his book, *Effective Teaching and Mentoring,* with the sentence, "Mentoring is a slippery concept." [2] Let me offer a definition to use in this book that I hope will make our approach more secure than slippery: "Mentoring is the work of a mentor to assist a mentorand's (the person being mentored) personal growth, skill development and role socialization so the mentorand can be more effective and achieve organizational and career goals."

The origin of the word "mentor" is Homer's *Odyssey* in which

---

[2] Laurent Daloz, *Effective Teaching and Mentoring* (San Francisco: Jossey-Bass Publishers, 1990), p. ix.

Odysseus departs to the war of the siege of Troy and leaves his son, Telemachus, in the hands of a guardian, Mentor.

Education and business is emphasizing mentoring now. School administrators are pairing new teachers with experienced teachers in mentoring programs in public schools. Field educators are using the term "mentor" to replace previous names such as supervisor. Some corporations have created mentor programs for young persons entering their employ. Where a corporation does not have such a program, some new employees have sought a mentor to guide them through the corporate maze.

Ministers often look back to their early years of ministry and realize that a home church pastor, the senior pastor in the church where they served as a staff member, or a relative in the ministry served as a mentor although there was not formal mentor agreement. Sometimes the supervisor in a student's field education program continues to relate to the minister long after graduation.

Mission agencies have not made much use of the term mentoring. The term might be more acceptable where a student or a recent seminary graduate engages in mission work. The term might be useful in foreign missions where a new missionary is appointed to work beside veteran missionaries. However, a seasoned minister may respond negatively to the word. An area mission director may work with many seasoned mission people where the relationship has traditionally been administrative and they perceive the word "mentor" to be a teacher-to-student relationship.

Mentor shares, with the word supervisor, the implication of an over/under relationship. The word supervisor implies an administrative relationship and the word mentor implies a learning relationship. However, both terms have outgrown their common usages.

Although the word "mentor" may not exactly describe official relationships, the process of mentoring occurs in good supervision described in my definition. There is the need for everyone to grow and the one charged with the responsibility for the work assists others in their personhood growth process and to obtain skills needed to do their tasks. Functionally, the supervisor serves a mentoring role.

Coach

A coach is a person responsible for developing players and a plan of action. Seminar participants have often suggested that the word "coach" might be a suitable word rather than supervisor. Americans are so immersed in sports that coach is an understandable term and more in favor than other alternatives especially, as some have suggested, if we use "player-coach" as the model. I believe many see coaching as more of a partnership than other models.

The coach develops a game plan and helps each player understand his or her role in the game plan. The coach analyzes how each person executes during the practice sessions and assigns players to their positions.

The term "coach" has gained favor recently in business where the traditional model of supervision and organization has been changed to the team approach especially in total quality management. Personnel are encouraged to think of themselves as the decision makers rather than supervisors and the coach is the facilitator of the team, not the traditional "boss."

I know of only a few mission agencies that have gone to total quality management and none to the team approach. Mission agencies still appoint personnel with supervisors responsible for people in their divisions or departments.

The coach approach is still an over/under relationship. I cannot imagine a player telling Vince Lombardi or Bear Bryant how to run the team. Nevertheless, a major task of any supervisor is to develop the persons involved in a task into a team.

No one word (mentor, supervisor, coach) adequately describes the work or the role of the supervisor in a mission system. The word "supervisor" may be the best word available. A supervisor is a person who takes or is given the responsibility to relate to people in order to achieve a goal or goals. A good supervisor will address the personhood issue among those who are on the team and move toward fulfilling the task responsibilities. While I will refer to supervision in this book, I will use the term "supervisor" to describe the person responsible for the supervising, mentoring and coaching.

MODELS OF SUPERVISORS

Where do we get our ideas of supervision? A former colleague of mine at Midwestern Seminary, Roy Woodruff, believes that we get our supervision style from our fathers. Whatever the source of our usual supervisory style, I hope that we can become conscious of our style and be adaptive enough to use the most helpful style in the various situations we face. We experience many different styles and, even if we get our usual style from our fathers, we probably are influenced by the styles we encounter.

While I will describe several styles, there is no "holy" style. I suggest the most righteous style is the one that best fits the situation we face.

Family

The first supervision we experience is in the family. When a child is born, the parents become supervisors. They decide what clothes he or she will wear and where the child will sleep. Later the child will voice choices about what to wear. As they become adolescents, they will choose which clothes to buy. As adults they will be self-directing. This style of supervision covers both personhood and task. Parents want their children to grow, mature, be healthy and productive.

Industry

The foreman is the supervisor in the factory shop. He or she oversees the work of the labor force so that it is the most productive. This type of supervision is task oriented. It is not a part of the work of the foreman to care for the personhood issues of the workers.

Business

The title of the supervisor in business may be manager, director or supervisor. The responsibility of this supervisor is to assign tasks and coordinate the work so that everything gets done. The business supervisor may serve as a mentor at times, helping people to understand corporate processes or how to do tasks. Traditionally the business supervisor does not get involved with personhood issues. However, the corporate world has begun to realize that the development of personnel is a good investment for them. Some corporations have sponsored "in house" seminars or sent their employees to seminars for personal growth.

Military

The military supervisor serves in a command system that makes supervision clear. The commanding officer gives orders upon which lower grade officers act. There is mentoring in the system since recruits must learn the military code of conduct and how to fulfill their responsibilities. The military chaplaincy is one way that personhood issues are addressed. However, the distinctive element about the military supervisor is the command system that focuses on tasks.

Craft

The guilds of the middle ages began using a supervisor system where a master craftsman would take an apprentice and teach him the trade (as far as I know, this was universally a male undertaking). When the apprentice had learned well enough, he made a sample of his craft and showed it for others to judge that he had achieved the status of "master." This is where we get the word "masterpiece." The major role of the master craftsman was mentor, teaching the apprentice how to do the craft.

Penal

The prison guard is the most easily identified supervisor in the penal model. The guard has the task of the security of the facility. The guard oversees the movement of the prisoners when they go to meals, work detail and recreation. The guard's supervision style is to use whatever force is necessary to maintain the discipline of the prisoners.

Orchestra

The orchestra conductor is the supervisor. The conductor's responsibility is to get the members of the orchestra to give his or her interpretation of a piece of music through the playing of their instruments. The conductor does not grab a violin and play the violin section of the music, then the oboe, then the trombone, etc. The conductor works with the musicians to produce a faithful interpretation of the music. The conductor is the coordinator of a series of musical tasks. The good conductor, especially with developing musicians, sometimes leads by coaching.

Marriage

Good married partners take care of one another. They work together to achieve their goals. One may be the supervisor with one role and the other a supervisor in another role. However, they are not interested only in tasks but one another's welfare. There may be times for each to mentor and coach the other.

Good supervisors are conscious of situations and choose a model of leading that fits the situation. The supervisor should examine whether he or she is depending on only one model of supervision. The best supervisors are flexible so they can relate to different situations which they face.

CHAPTER 3

SUPERVISORS

There are good and poor supervisors. The best supervisors have positive personal qualities and follow the proper roles that make them good supervisors.

QUALITIES OF GOOD SUPERVISORS

Bill and Carl, two missionaries, met at a retreat. Their conversation turned to comparisons of their supervisors. Since both had served with their supervisors for a brief period, neither could provide much detail. However, one spoke eloquently about his supervisor's work while the other spoke vehemently about his supervisor's shortcomings. What were the differences? How do you sort out what it takes to make a good supervisor?

Many books on supervision have reported surveys about the characteristics of good supervisors. Usually these have some characteristics in common and others are different. My interest is not supervision in general but the qualities of a good supervisor (mentor, leader, coach) in mission systems.

ART AND SCIENCE OF SUPERVISION

Supervision is both an art and a science. Throughout history there have been good intuitive supervisors. They have been able to respond appropriately to the situations they faced. Only recently have groups started to approach supervision as a discipline.

Art is doing things intuitively. Intuitive supervisors follow their hunches. Good supervisors seem to have the right hunches. We speak of a person playing the piano by "ear." This person has an "intuitive" ability to play without the science of notes being written on a page.

Science uses specific, disciplined steps. While some people are natural supervisors by intuition, some people need help in developing into supervisors. Others could be better supervisors with help. Psychologists began to examine the make up of supervisors a few decades ago and determined how they could help people become supervisors. They have taught persons methods and helped their supervision.

Just as people have been unable to play the piano by "ear" but have learned to be good pianists through the science of music, there are people who would not have attained good supervision without the science of supervision. When people use science, they follow specific activities that help them reach their goals. Even intuitive supervisors may do well but have no disciplined pattern to help them evaluate how they are doing.

Regardless of the helpfulness of science, there is always the subjective element in supervision. Value judgements will have to be made. This is important because people cannot be transformed into things to be quantified.

There are some qualities of supervisors in mission systems that help them be effective.

Faith

Supervisors should be persons of faith. We probably take for granted that the mission supervisor will have faith; however, this element is too important not to mention. The supervisor is not a person with a bag of tricks which he or she passes on to others but a person who has internalized Christian values and graces. This spirituality reflects the image of God.

Health

A mission supervisor needs to be healthy emotionally as well as spiritually. As some diseases are contagious, emotional illness is also contagious. Where the mission supervisor is emotionally ill, people nearby will become ill. Healthy people will be isolated (or will isolate themselves to preserve their emotional health). We minister with ourselves as well as our programs. If we are emotionally unhealthy, we will be destructive to people and eventually to mission systems. The unhealthy person may be charismatic and attract many people. This makes the emotionally unhealthy person more of a threat.

Dr. Don Gardner, a hospital chaplain, did a Doctor of Ministry project attempting to find the differences in recidivism rates among people in a mental clinic. He compared people from healthy congregations, unhealthy congregations and those with no religious connections. (He defined healthy congregations as those emphasizing love, acceptance and forgiveness. He defined unhealthy congregations as those emphasizing judgment, wrath and guilt.) Dr. Gardner found persons from unhealthy congregations had the highest rates of recidivism—even higher than those who had no church connections. It is not enough for supervisors to be religious; they need to be healthy. A neurotic supervisor will create other neurotics.

Caring

My definition of supervision included, "The development of a support system," so support and caring are necessary for good mission supervisors. There may be reasons why supervisors make mistakes, but there is no reason not to care. Caring is not determined by education, age, intelligence or experience; it is the spontaneous reaction of a regenerate soul.

Courage

The Foreign Mission Board assigned a young woman to work in a mission institution overseas. It was a Muslim country so there were many restrictions on the activities of women. The young missionary woman apparently had some unresolved adolescent rebellion issues. The local mission administrator complained to the mission supervisor about her behavior with the students. However, no one had the courage to intervene.

The young woman became pregnant and had to return home.

Courage is a quality for living, not dying in battle. Courage faces hard tasks rather than avoiding them. Supervisors often take the course of least resistance, believing that "everything will turn out all right in the end." As in the case cited above, it doesn't turn out all right. It takes courage to intervene in difficult situations rather than let them "run their course." The courageous supervisor may save everyone from difficulty by interventive action, but everyone may blame the supervisor. However, when courage is called for, failing to act brings serious consequences. We will never know what would have happened to the young missionary in the case above had one of the supervisors intervened.

A mission supervisor has to have the courage to lead, err, confront and affirm. J. W. Thomas, in his Bi/Polar system of psychology, changed his terminology so that what he once called "risking," he now calls "couraging." [1] A good supervisor has the courage to make value judgements and confront people.

We often think of courage only in terms of doing, but our doing comes out of our being. One of Paul Tillich's most influential books was *The Courage to Be*. Supervisors need the courage to be authentic. Where there is inadequate authenticity, supervisors will use intimidation or manipulation.

Growth

The axiom is, "Whenever something stops growing, it is dying or dead." The mission supervisor needs to grow because the supervisor is in the business of helping others grow. The supervisor is on a pilgrimage and he or she must push on, never resting on past achievements.

---

[1] See J. W. Thomas, *Bi/Polar: A Positive Way of Understanding People* (Richardson, Texas: Bi/Polar, Inc., 1978), p. 26 for Thomas' earlier use of risking.

Model

The supervisor leads by example. As an illustration, the best way a supervisor can motivate is by being motivated. Energy in the supervisor creates energy in others. Mission supervisors don't always have the same task assignments as those whom they work with, but they can still be an example of commitment, discipline, work, caring and energy.

Authority

Dr. Ernie White, late professor of church administration at Southern Baptist Theological Seminary, used to define authority as divine, institutional or personal.[2] The misuse of authority is to claim the wrong type of authority in a situation. We often think of the misuse of authority as being heavy handed, but it is as much a misuse of authority to neglect it. The good use of authority is not to use it for self-serving purposes.

Preparation

The difference between an effective and ineffective supervisor is often preparation. Supervisors need training in supervision. Supervisors do an injustice to persons in their care if they do not get supervisory training to help them with the tasks of supervision. When a supervisor has a supervisory, mentoring or coaching conference, the supervisor will usually be effective to the degree of preparation made.

Insight

Good supervision requires an inner vision to understand what is happening in the surroundings and to others. Dr. Art Carlson was a chaplain at Trinity Lutheran Hospital in Kansas City

---

[2] Ernest White, "The Supervision of Doctor of Ministry Students" in *Spirituality, Ministry, and Field Education* (The Association for Theological Field Education, 1986), pp. 236-238.

when he lost his sight in mid-adult life. He continued to serve as a C.P.E. supervisor because his inner vision was more important to his work than his physical sight. The supervisor needs insight into the human heart. He or she needs to know when someone is hurting.

Communication

Good communication is essential for supervisors. My wife reminds me that she can't read my mind. Neither can people read the supervisor's mind. The regular supervisory conferences are times to communicate clearly, directly and fully.

Listening is a crucial part of communication. The supervisor should make sure that he or she hears what people are saying by asking clarifying, non-judgmental questions as part of listening. Supervisors should listen for the unspoken as well as the spoken.

Flexibility

Life situations are always changing, and good supervisors will be flexible to meet the changes. There are few absolutes but many relativities. While we guard absolutes, we can be flexible on relative issues.

Perspective

Keeping things in a proper perspective is a delicate art. When a person is "in the trenches," it is easy to lose perspective. Others may be in their own trenches. The good supervisor will have the perspective of the whole situation rather than only his or her situation. I worry when I see someone who has lost his or her sense of humor even in difficult situations. I fear that the person has lost perspective, along with his or her sense of humor.

Relational

Perhaps relating to people is the most important for the

supervisor. It may not be the most important for a cardiac surgeon, but for a mission supervisor, it is essential. We work with people, not inanimate objects.

You may want to write in some qualities you have observed among good supervisors you have met. I hope you will examine how these impact your role as a supervisor.

ROLES OF SUPERVISORS

A few years ago I was the supervisor of a doctoral candidate who had been a friend since college. Once he asked, "Are you trying to be my supervisor, my friend or my pastor?" It was a good question because supervisors need to define and become conscious of roles.

Inappropriate Supervisory Roles

Supervisors have specific and appropriate roles consistent with their agencies' systems. If the supervisor moves out of the appropriate role, he or she has forfeited the supervisor's role.

A good supervisor is not an administrator. While a supervisor may have administrative responsibilities, he or she is a supervisor, not an administrator. A supervisor supervises people, but an administrator administrates a program. The supervisor may have more experience, expertise and comfort in administrating than in supervising. This means he or she must give attention not to slip into the role of administrator.

Bob Kelly, director of missions of a large metropolitan area Baptist association, has several persons on his staff. When asked about his style of supervising one of the members of his staff, he replied, "I work with her in coordinating the calendar and going over the budget." From conversations with the staff member, I knew that she needed someone to help her concerning the direction of her ministry and to give her affirmation. She was probably more capable of handling the calendar and budget than any other facet of her job. The role which the director of missions chose was that of administrator rather than supervisor. While the administrator's role was a legitimate one for the director of missions, he was forfeiting his role and neglecting the real need.

The supervisor is not a bishop. Even in denominations which have bishops, their primary role is usually that of administrator more than the kind of supervisor addressed in this book. However, people from the Free Church tradition often identify "supervision" with "bishop." A bishop has ultimate responsibility for all of the congregations in a diocese, while the supervisor in a Free Church tradition does not. The supervisor is not a bishop who controls the congregation or the minister. The word for bishop in the pastoral epistles in the New Testament was *episcopos* meaning "overseer." [3] The supervisor does not serve as the bishop-overseer of a congregation or the pastor. The only things possibly described as "overseeing" in a supervisor's role are the responsibilities contained in the covenant that are agreed upon by the congregation, the supervisor and the supervisee.

The supervisor is not a therapist. If a person faces emotional difficulties, he or she may need therapy, but the supervisor who tries to serve as a therapist only confuses the supervisor role. Supervisors of mission personnel require specialized skills in ministry, but most mission supervisors lack special training and expertise in psychotherapy. Hopefully, the supervisors of mission personnel will have enough skills to recognize psychological problems and refer the person who needs help to a skilled psychotherapist.

The mission supervisor is not a pastor to mission personnel. The supervisor may be a pastor (or previously a pastor) and have pastoral skills; however, the roles of supervisor and pastor are separate roles. When the supervisor sees that the mission personnel need a pastor, he or she should exercise care not to mix the roles. Since mission personnel often serve as pastors and do not have a pastor readily available, it is natural for them to turn to the supervisor for pastoral ministry. When it becomes necessary for a supervisor to provide pastoral ministry, the

---

[3] 1 Timothy 3:1.

supervisor should redefine the relationship and step out of the supervisor's role.

Appropriate Supervisor Roles

The supervisor functions in several roles. Each related agency creates a role for the supervisor. The director of missions in a Baptist association, for example, functions in several roles. The role differs as the director relates to congregations in the association, the state Baptist convention, the Home Mission Board and the Sunday School Board, not to mention the local Chamber of Commerce and Kiwanis Club.

The mission supervisor overseas has another set of agencies. These agencies include the Foreign Mission Board, the mission on the field of service, the national Baptist group as well as an association and local church. Additionally the mission supervisor overseas relates to embassies of the United States and the host country. "Go and make disciples" sounds simple at first, but the supervisor has to fulfill many roles to achieve the evangelistic goal.

Changing Roles

There is an axiom that when there is a change, there is loss. When mission personnel change roles, they usually face a sense of loss. When students leave the seminary to go to a mission task, they face the loss of an educational community, their close friends, the highly structured academic model of classes and curriculum. This is one reason why the Foreign Mission Board requires two years of ministry service after seminary prior to appointing a person for overseas ministry. Although students look forward to independence, they will be lost without the structure a supervision system provides when they become missionaries.

A foreign mission supervisor wrote: "When the person who has never been outside of the USA first arrives, often their expectations of life in another country is very idealistic and naive." [4] It is impossible for a person to imagine what life will be like away from previous support systems such as culture, family and familiar institutions as well as language that is not a native tongue.

The Foreign Mission Board appointed an older couple to an overseas mission. They had served their last church nearly twenty years. The supervisor of the overseas mission met them and helped them settle in their house to begin language study. A week later they informed the supervisor that they were resigning and returning to the United States. The wife realized that the missionary role was not appropriate for her. It was the first time she had ever examined her role other than being a part of her husband's role. She was not able to cope with the role change.

Robert Duncan served as pastor of a Baptist congregation in a small Texas town. Baptists were the dominant religious group in the area. In fact, Duncan's church was the largest church in town. Since he had been there four years, almost everybody in town knew him. He accepted a mission appointment to go to a city in the North and become the first pastor of a new chapel. Lutherans and Roman Catholics were the dominant religious groups in the northern city. Few people had ever known a Baptist; what they knew they had learned from the pages of *Newsweek* and *Time* magazines. Only a few Southern Baptist congregations existed in the entire state.   The nearest one to Duncan was more than seventy-five miles away.

He discovered that people seemed more matter of fact and less emotional about everything, including religion, than Texans. In Texas, he had buried half the town's people who died, had married half the young people, had been invited to preach or pray at all the baccalaureate exercises at the high school. He had been sought out to join the Lions Club. As a mission pastor in the northern city, no one knew him or invited him to participate in civic affairs.

---

[4]From Papers on Supervision supplied by the Southern Baptist Foreign Mission Board.

Robert Duncan returned to Texas after a short time.   He missed his role as "town parson," thus experiencing a great sense of personal loss. A good supervisor could have helped him make that change by helping him see what was happening and leading him to develop a new, satisfying role.

Changing roles may bring fear. A state director of church and community ministries once confided his feelings about his recent change from the pastoral role. He was afraid he could not "measure up" in his new role. This fear did not come externally but came from within himself. In his previous role, he knew what was expected; in the new role, he was less certain. Fear can immobilize. Fear can prevent a person from "measuring up." Fear can also cause a person to become hyperactive. Charged with the great energy of fear, they compulsively perform tasks, often ineffectively.

Role change can generate misunderstanding. For example, supervisors may fail to understand role change and continue to work out of the previous roles. In a move from a pastorate to becoming a supervisor in a denominational agency, the supervisor may still devote energies to the previously familiar roles rather than the new roles.

Each of these situations can be handled in a number of ways. In the most effective approach, the mission supervisor and the mission personnel will consciously address their roles, explicitly define them and work within those definitions.

Personhood and Task in the Supervisor's Role

A primary consideration for the mission supervisor is awareness of task and personhood issues since the supervisor's role includes both task and personhood. This is especially important where the supervisor serves in a system that has not provided for personhood to be part of the supervision.

This role is made more difficult in a culture (or sub-culture) that is task oriented. The supervisor has to go against the grain of prevailing behavior and thinking. The covenant will have to spell out personhood issues as well as task issues. The supervisor can help the process by examining the covenant frequently to determine how personhood goals are being addressed.

SUMMARY

Roles are always present. It will help if the supervisor works with mission personnel to express what these are. The good supervisor will monitor relationships to determine what roles he or she serves.

CHAPTER 4

ELEMENTS OF SUPERVISION

ACCOUNTABILITY

We are all accountable to God. We are also accountable to others: Our spouse, civil authority, family, friends, institutions to which we belong. We are not accountable equally to these, but we are definitely accountable.

Every system requires accountability. Without it, the system lacks integrity and is unlikely to fulfill its mission. When money is involved, it is rare when there is no accountability. Boards and trustees are elected to ensure accountability. Accountability is an essential element of supervision. Without it, supervision can offer no support. The supervisor is the one charged with being accountable and holding supervisees accountable.

When a missionary takes a position, he or she becomes accountable to the people who appoint and provide financial support. Because people are ultimately accountable to God, the missionary should determine at the beginning if the accountability demanded by others interferes with or contravenes accountability to God. There is a human need for accountability. A person who expects to be held accountable will usually meet expectations. For example, if a professor gives pop tests each day over reading assignments, students are likely to read each day.

Accountability should be fair. Supervisors should explain accountability when making covenants with their missionaries.

Expectations of accountability stated up front will let mission personnel know how the process works and when reports are due. Accountability relates to the covenant. Supervisors should hold missionaries accountable for responsibilities according to their covenants and job descriptions. No surprises.

Forms of Accountability

The main forms of accountability are written and oral. Each has advantages. Many supervisors prefer to use a combination of written and oral reports in accountability.

Written. A written form may be narrative in style to give the personnel an opportunity to elaborate on what has happened. This provides opportunities to describe ministries in ways that might not be on a standardized report form.

The journal provides a day-to-day reporting. It includes activities and reflections on activities. While the journal is more than a time log, it may show the time invested.

Some agencies have standardized, written report forms. These usually take less time to prepare. However, it is difficult to report personhood issues on standardized forms or to report items of interest to the missionary. The standardized report forms serve the purpose of the mission agency (such as the number of baptisms).

Written forms of accountability are formal and provide structured evaluation. This is important in the present litigation-prone American society. If termination becomes necessary, the supervisor may need documentation covering an extended period to justify termination. Written forms of accountability are also important for personnel review related to salary or rank change or new responsibilities. A supervisor who keeps a notebook on each person finds the notations provide helpful information for, and gives validity to, annual evaluations.

Written forms stimulate reflection. People are more likely to reflect when writing than when only speaking. Since many write a first draft and type a second draft, reflection is built into the process.

Oral. The oral form of accountability is usually quicker and takes less preparation time. The oral method allows the supervisor to look the other person in the eye and react immediately to responses. The supervisors can ask for more information, test hunches and probe further into matters. Often supervisors rely on body language when they evaluate a supervisee. The oral method is more flexible since supervisors can ask questions spontaneously about specific situations rather than the generic questions often asked in written forms.

The oral method has disadvantages. It is only as good as the supervisor's insight and courage. Supervisors may not be skilled at asking questions. Some supervisors have series of questions, but these relinquish the advantages of the oral method. The supervisor may know questions that he or she needs to ask but be too timid to ask them.

When accountability is oral, the supervisor needs to make detailed notes during the interview and enter them in the person's file. The wise supervisor will show these notes to the supervisees and ask them to sign that they have read them. Signing does not mean that they agree with what the supervisor has written.

Combination. Often the best approach is a combination of oral and written methods. A supervisor can give a missionary any form an agency requires, give instructions about the form and ask for additional written information. After reading responses, the supervisor and missionary can schedule a conference. In the conference the supervisor can discuss the written form but also give opportunity for oral responses.

Times of Accountability

The covenant should name times of accountability. Times of major accountability may be when the covenant is fulfilled, during an annual evaluation or when a position is terminated. Although there may be a schedule for formal evaluations, accountability is ongoing. Each conference the supervisor holds with the missionary is a time of accountability. The missionary should know at the end of each conference if the supervisor is pleased.

Standards of Accountability

Mission agencies set standards for accountability. Where several mission agencies sponsor a single placement, there can be confusion. The supervisor can reduce the confusion by minimizing the paper work and interpreting the materials so the missionary can provide information efficiently. The supervisor may have additional standards beyond (but not contrary to) those of the mission agency. The supervisor must be fair and let the missionary know this up front and not expect more than is reasonable.

Missionaries may disagree with the standards set by the mission agencies. When these standards violate a missionary's principles and conscience, the missionary should not accept appointment. If the missionary thinks that the standards are merely ineffective or obsolete, he or she may work to help the agency recognize the limitations. Accountability by mission agencies is not the "great white throne" but, when done well, it is a way supervisors can help missionaries and agencies.

ACCOUNTABILITY
THROUGH EVALUATION

Evaluation may be threatening, but it is necessary. While ministers may not set up evaluation committees, the congregation evaluates them each time they preach. My friend, Fred Pryor, says, "The only thing worse than finding out what somebody thinks about you is not finding out. You may find out when it is too late to do anything about it." Often ministers do not receive evaluation until it is too late. People may be nice until tensions reach a critical point and by then relationships have broken down. The minister needs to test reality through feedback. Supervisors should help mission personnel feel comfortable with receiving feedback so that they will continue to seek evaluation throughout their ministries.

What Is the Goal of Evaluation?

Evaluation provides feedback to mission personnel so they can feel affirmed by their victories, or make appropriate corrections. Evaluation also fulfills the need of systems for accountability. We would not want to be a part of a system so irresponsible that there is no accountability. Karl Barth once said that judgment is an act of the grace of God. Without judgment there is no possibility of failure and without the possibility of failure, there can be no victory.

What Does the Supervisor Evaluate?

The covenant is the basis of evaluation. It guides the supervisor in the process and provides the issues for evaluation. The evaluation may involve the mission personnel's knowledge, skill, personhood or performance. Educational institutions have sophisticated ways of measuring knowledge acquisition, but there are few adequate ways for evaluating skills, personhood and performance. Despite good skills, mission personnel may have psychological blocks that hinder performance. Good supervisors help mission personnel detect the cause of unacceptable performance. Supervisors and mission personnel perhaps can determine whether poor skills are the cause in order to remedy the situation. On the other hand, personhood issues may cause poor performance.

Who Evaluates Supervisees?

The mission system has policies about evaluation. Mission personnel have the right to know who will be evaluating them. (I remember walking into my Ph.D. oral exam and finding that new professors, who had not read my thesis, had been appointed to my oral committee.) The local supervisor receives reports and observes the mission personnel so he or she is in the best position to evaluate. A shared supervision situation may require team evaluation with other persons participating.

Mission personnel can evaluate themselves because they know their inner feelings as no one else. Peers may provide valuable evaluation. People often accept evaluation from peers when they will accept it from no one else. Laypersons can also provide evaluation. They have a unique perspective and are the real and final human judges of mission personnel. Others may also be evaluators because of their position with agencies. These usually draw upon data submitted to them. Their evaluations often compare outside data to the agency's expectations.

When Will Evaluation Occur?

Evaluation happens the first time we see someone. We judge a person as bright or dull, ambitious or lazy, kind or hateful. Obviously we would be in error to depend upon first impressions. Supervisors need more structured evaluations. Evaluation should take place throughout the relationship. Every time they meet, the supervisor should indicate whether the person is fulfilling expectations. Formal evaluations should not hold major surprises. A formal evaluation at the midpoint in the covenant relationship opens the possibility for any midpoint correction. By waiting until midpoint, the supervisor has time to check out hunches. The final evaluation should be highly structured with the supervisor and mission personnel evaluating performance in light of the covenant.

How Will I Prepare for and Conduct an Evaluation?

Supervisors may feel a sense of panic at having to evaluate another person. They may seek evaluation forms. While these are helpful, none is entirely adequate. It is difficult to design one form to accommodate many ministry settings. While panic does not help, the supervisor will recognize the evaluation is important enough to have anxiety.

One evaluation method involves a journal that reviews the significant performance and accomplishments. The supervisor and the supervisee review the journal periodically.

Another method is the narrative report, an in-depth written evaluation in narrative form that reflects the supervisor's assessment of work, growth and relationships. This type of evaluation allows the supervisor to report on any type of ministry setting.

For the formal evaluation session, the supervisor requests that the supervisee prepare written evaluations, based on their cove-

nant. The evaluation sessions will address performance, super-
visor/supervisee relationship, accomplishments, work in the light
of criteria set out in the covenant and future plans.   Are they
merely going through the motions to fulfill the covenant or
attempting to accomplish something? A good evaluation session
makes it possible for personnel to leave with a clear understanding of the supervisor's evaluation and future expectations.

What Is a Grid Evaluation?

A grid evaluation provides a series of issues by which a
supervisor can evaluate the function of personnel. Everyone has
a mental grid but, an external grid gives the parties in evaluation a common system in the evaluation process. A grid evaluation makes evaluation more "scientific" by drawing a profile
with data collected about the mission personnel. The supervisor
should review the mission personnel's experiences from personal observations, lay evaluation, self-evaluation, peer evaluation, supervisor reports, ministry journals and ministry action
contacts according to a grid which should reveal patterns of
performance. The important element in this type of evaluation
is to discover patterns. Individual experiences are not as important as patterns since patterns usually continue. Supervisors
should address counter-productive patterns and affirm productive patterns.

While grid system is a helpful "scientific" tool, supervisors
cannot escape making value judgments.   Their value judgments
are not absolute but tentative and serve as a basis of discussion.

Whatever the evaluation form, it is the content that counts.
The content consists of universal issues: knowledge, skills,
personhood and performance. Ministry performance is not
mechanical; it is conditioned by the mission personnel's human-
ity. The good supervisor will figure out what factors (knowledge, skills, personhood) are enabling or inhibiting the mission
personnel's performance. Issues of personhood are usually the
most threatening and nebulous, but they are closer to where the
person really lives. We may sense that something is there, but
not be able to name it. Once we name it, we may be able to

deal with it. Below is a list of related issues that a supervisor may use in grid evaluation.

1. Work. Different people have different energy levels. A good question is, "What is the mission personnel's capacity for work?" Supervisors should observe the work level expended on different tasks. Is more energy invested in visitation than in sermon preparation? Does a missionary spend more energy with nationals than with fellow missionaries? Does a hobby consume more energy than visitation? Do certain tasks take more energy than necessary?

It is important to examine the meaningfulness of work. Mission personnel may find work meaningless and invest minimal time. Workaholics may be neurotically driven to work since they have to do so much to get satisfaction. Meaningfulness extends to the kind of work they do. They may only invest in dramatic or grandiose projects and find no meaning in the routine. Others may be locked into the routine and limit themselves to "housekeeping" work. If a situation intimidates a person, he or she may avoid it by working inordinately on "housekeeping" work. Some mission personnel work only on their agenda rather than invest in the needs of others. How mission personnel sustain a work level (especially without outside stimuli) will be a helpful indicator of maturity.

2. Authority. Supervisors need to note how mission personnel handle authority. Are they rebellious toward authority or adaptive to authority figures? How do they react in the presence of authority figures? Do they avoid authority or seek out authority figures when the situation does not demand or suggest it? Do they have a sense of their own authority and do they claim it? Ministers use three forms of authority: official, calling and personal. Supervisors should notice whether mission personnel work through their personal authority rather than their calling as a minister or if they rely upon official authority rather than exerting personal authority.

3. Initiating. Initiating describes the ability to take the lead to start projects, solve problems and develop relationships. Overly dependent people may have difficulties in this area. Some mission personnel initiate within a strong, familiar structure. Others initiate action where no structure exists or even in the face of resistance. Some mission personnel initiate regarding organizational matters. Others successfully initiate personal relationships but have difficulty with organizations. The ability to initiate overcomes many problems. Passive missionary personnel, who wait for things to happen, cannot effectively exercise their gifts. Mission personnel who always have to be the ones to take initiative also create problems.

4. Sex roles. Ministry personnel need to be aware of and comfortable with appropriate sex roles. American society is facing change in sex roles and mission personnel cannot escape this. Sex roles are especially sensitive issues in every country. Foreign missionaries have to learn to respect those roles that are cultural rather than moral. It is important whether they feel more comfortable working with women or men.

It will also be important to see how mission personnel use the sex role issue prevalent in society in their work. How do they handle it when their own sex role belief runs counter to those of the people being served? How does it affect the working relationship when the mission personnel (or supervisor) with which one works is of the opposite sex?

5. Theological reflection. Through theological reflection, you find theological principles inherent in and appropriate to experiences. Every action has theological ramifications. Theological reflection attempts to integrate theological and biblical knowledge, applying them to human experiences.

Theological reflection also examines our confessed theology, our theological theory and our consistency in theological presuppositions. When we find we are inconsistent, we can either change our actions in the light of our confessed theology or reexamine their confessed theology. At times, we must claim the hiatus between their confessed theology and our actions, holding the two in tension until we resolve the paradox.

6. Investment awareness. People have emotional and personal investment in people, causes, ideas or memories. We may express these investments by monetary means, time or emotional identification. Supervisors need to find out if the mission personnel are aware of their own investments and if they appreciate the investments of other people.

7. Power structures. We need to recognize formal and

informal power structures. We need to know their inherent dangers to our role as a change agent. We will need to accept and appropriately use our power. The minister has three sources of power: official, call and personal. A minister may refuse to act unless empowered by official action. Others may try to solve all problems on a personal basis of friendship or charm.

8. Personal structure. People have an inner structure. It may be rigid and get in the way of relating to others or to an organization. It may be unresponsive to change. The inner structure may lack form so it cannot resist agenda set on it by others or develop personal discipline.

9. Agendas. Mission personnel should be aware of their own agenda. Missionaries have arrived at their field of service and faced immediate conflict with the mission setting because they came with a different agenda. They also need to be able to read the agendas of others.

10. Covenants. Covenant is a metaphorical expression for the content of relationships based on expectations people bring to those relationships. This includes formal, informal and tacit covenants. Mission personnel profit as they can determine existing covenants and raise to consciousness the covenants that are never spelled out. They need to know the covenants which situations automatically impose upon people. Ministers often have difficulties because they do not recognize the covenants which they have inadvertently made, which others impose on them or which their role creates.

11. Conflict. Mission personnel have to deal with conflict situations so they need to be able to identify elements of conflict and develop methods for dealing with it creatively. Supervisors should test how mission personnel deal with their anger created by conflict.

12. Transitions. People in transition call for pastoral care. Supervisors should evaluate how much mission personnel are aware of multi-transition dynamics and how they use rites to facilitate life transitions. Since mission personnel undergo transitions, supervisors need to examine how mission personnel handle change. Changes may be intellectual as personnel face new theological ideas and cultural challenges; or personal, as they marry and have children; or as they move to a new ministry role.

Geographical transition is also important. A person can expect cultural shock as he or she moves from the South to New England or from American to Asia. The loss of health and the death of a loved one are transitions many face during missionary service.

13. Loss. Mission personnel should be aware of the dimensions and types of losses that occur in human experience. The supervisor needs to examine how sensitive mission personnel are to different aspects of loss and how they minister to people undergoing these kinds of experiences. Mission personnel experiencing loss through accidents, impaired health, death of family members or romantic losses may expect assistance by their supervisors.

14. Discipline. The supervisor should determine if mission personnel are in charge of their time, energy and ministry resources.

15. Anxiety. Supervisors observe mission personnel in crises and in everyday experiences. Anxiety may block a person's ability to function. Overreaction due to anxiety may indicate that he or she has a serious problem to deal with before the mission personnel experience trauma or psychological breakdown. Anxiety is a natural reaction to situations and can serve to heighten a person's attention. Too little anxiety may be a signal that there is not enough creative challenge in the assignments.

16. Self-identity. Every adult needs to develop his or her self-identity. Because people are dynamic, problems occur in self-perception or self-identity. Mission personnel have many different roles (child, parent, friend, minister, employee, husband or wife) and these influence self-identity. As we change, we usually have to reexamine our self-identity.

17. Ministry identity. Mission personnel need to integrate their self-identity and ministry identity. Often ministers subjugate one identity to the other. Some deny personal identity to take on a ministry identity. Others will try to be "authentic" human beings and shy away from a ministry identity that will make them uncomfortable in the ministry role. Some will be able to use their ministry role while remaining conscious of their personal self-identity.

18. Affirmation.   Supervisors need to find the source of affirmation for mission personnel and their ability to accept healthy affirmation. Mission personnel should be able to affirm others freely. A significant part of ministry is blessing others.

19. Resistance.   As supervisors meet resistance in mission personnel, they can discover the source and determine whether resistance is a response to reality. They should look for the patterns in resistance: do they resist people or ideas? Supervisors should also discover how mission personnel deal with the resistance they meet.

20. Defenses.   Supervisors can probe the defense mechanisms of the mission personnel. If specific mechanisms are unneeded, the supervisor may be able to help the person eliminate the use of the defense mechanism.

21. Personal strengths.   The supervisor should find out whether mission personnel can identify and own their personal strengths.

22. Definition of issues.   How well do mission personnel define issues? They should be able to articulate the issues in language appropriate to the nature of the issues as well as in "God language."

23. Ability to focus.   Supervisors should examine the mission personnel's ability to focus attention and efforts on issues without diffusing their energies that could hinder them from bringing their powers to bear significantly upon issues of life and ministry.

24. Functioning in nonstructured situations.   Mission personnel will need to function outside their structured roles of preaching, teaching, etc. Can they initiate in nonstructured role situations as well as in structured situations?

25. Functioning at different levels.   Functioning at different levels involves people at different religious, intellectual and social levels. Mission personnel need to function with non-clergy as well as clergy; in nonreligious scenarios as well as religious structures. Also how does a person function at different intimacy levels?

26. Religious language.   Supervisors need to be aware of mission personnel's investment in and use of religious language. The person may be overly dependent upon religious language. Some may use it to avoid sensitive issues. Others may feel uncomfortable in a ministry role and, as a result, avoid religious language and people who use religious language.

27. Intellectualizing. Some people intellectualize rather than act. Some ministers prefer to explain why a situation occurs rather than intervene in the situation.

28. Spiritualizing. Some mission personnel interpret all experiences in "God language." They offer divine or demonic answers to all human experiences. Supervisors need to evaluate these tendencies and how well they are in touch with reality.

29. Spiritual formation. Supervisors can evaluate the stage of the spiritual developmental process of the mission personnel and help them integrate it with vocational life. A religious history may be helpful to determine spiritual development.

30. Perception of reality. Supervisors need to observe how mission personnel perceive reality. Do they act on the basis of reality or fantasy? Because of their presuppositions, naivete, anxiety, depression or immature judgment, they may distort reality. Those completely out of touch with reality may need therapy.

31. Internalized direction. Mission personnel may have internalized their sense of direction or it may emanate from archaic parent tapes or from external pressures. Take into account whether mission personnel are too dependent on the supervisor or on other structures. Eventually mission personnel may not have supervisors and will have to determine their individual course of action. Others may be far from their supervisors when they have to take action.

32. Risk. Risk involves the ability to move into areas where the outcome is uncertain for ministry, the institution or the person. Examine the mission personnel's willingness to become vulnerable and to move with intentionality and initiative. An examination of risking will demonstrate what is so significant that they are willing to risk for it.

33. Responding to failure. The patterns in response to failure may show that persons set themselves up to fail. People may follow a cycle from failure to anger to depression. The rare persons who seemingly never fail may face serious difficulties if or when they do experience failure.

34. Revealing of self. How well can mission personnel reveal themselves? Some "spill" themselves inappropriately either to people whom they hardly know or to persons who might utilize such information to hurt them. Others are so rigid they are unable to reveal anything significant about themselves.

35. Awareness of ministry contexts. We never minister in a vacuum. Contexts include family, congregation, the larger community of faith, secular community, government agencies and their confessional groups. It is easy to focus on one dimension and not be aware of all the publics to which we relate.

36. Integration of theory and practice. Mission personnel serve with a theology. They should be able to integrate theology and practice, by acting (and understanding action) in light of their theory. This integration is known as "praxis."

37. Personal relating. The supervisor may help mission personnel determine patterns of relating. Are they abrasive, flattering, loving or hateful? Do they relate as parents, adults or children? How intimate are their relationships?

This grid contains personhood issues. Each setting may develop a grid of skill issues such as preaching, evangelism, church starting and pastoral care. Supervisors who become familiar with this grid will become sensitive to and insightful into issues during conference times or reading reports. However, the supervisor may find it helpful to go over these with mission personnel.

CHAPTER 5

THE SUPERVISORY PROCESS

Two mission supervisors attending a workshop discussed how they relate to mission personnel. The first expressed an intense desire to know where his supervisee was at all times because he (the supervisor) was responsible for what happened on that mission field. He described daily meetings with his supervisee and related that they never met less than twice a week. The second supervisor smiled. "I don't have that much time to give to the job," he said, "and I feel that my man is a competent professional. I tell him to come to me if he runs into any problem. Otherwise, I leave him alone."

These supervisors exercise two distinct kinds of supervision. Which is correct?

Many factors determine the kind of supervision. It relates to personality, experience and our sense of security. In the opening illustration, the first supervisor may be operating out of his insecurity, keeping tight control. The second supervisor seems more secure, allowing more freedom. However, he may be as insecure as the first, if he refuses to face conflict and closes his eyes to needs of mission personnel.

Mission personnel represent another variable in the illustration. Perhaps the first supervisor is responsible for young and inexperienced personnel with no more than average ability. The second may be working with well-trained, stable and experienced personnel with a good track record. Geographical distance between supervisor and mission personnel also affects a situation.

If Roy Woodruff is correct and we tend to supervise the way

we were fathered, that may be the answer to different supervision styles. Every kind of supervision is not equally effective. One kind of supervision may "feel" more natural but fail to be effective. The supervisor can examine various styles to discover which fits his or her personality the best and which are the most effective with particular mission personnel in a specific setting.

STYLES OF SUPERVISION

When I use "supervisor" and "supervision" in this book, I refer to the work of the support person of mission personnel that blends the ideas of mentor, leader and coach. If I were describing supervision in a general sense, I would present different categories.

There are three basic supervision styles: direct, shared and tacit.

Direct Supervision

Supervisors who have a need for strong control use direct supervision. Supervisors using this style make decisions and expect compliance. This style can be seen in military and industry. It has the advantage of everyone knowing the chain of command. A good communicator can make responsibilities clear in the direct style. However, when ideas start from the top, it is hard to create ownership in others. It is not difficult to see that this approach retards team building. Also, ideas come from farthest point of their implementation.

Shared Supervision

Shared supervision suggests that there is more than one supervisor involved in the supervision process. This style is realistic in the Free Church tradition where no hierarchy exists. Several entities may be involved with the work of mission personnel. The Home Mission Board, a state convention, an association and a local church may work together to start a mission church. The Foreign Mission Board works through national missions and relates to national conventions and local churches. Shared supervision is a reality!

Shared supervision has the advantage of multiple resources (finances, personnel, ideas, influence) from the various entities. Many mission efforts would not have succeeded without multiple resources. Shared supervision has some dangers too. People may play "games" with one another.   Some who have been evaluating supervision among mission personnel have discovered that it is particularly important to create a covenant in shared supervision. The second important ingredient these observers have found is the direct relationship of regular communication among the supervisors and positive supervision results.

Tacit Supervision

Tacit supervision involves the denial of a supervision role by a supervisor who, nevertheless, exercises supervision.   The supervision may be expressed as covert expectations that certain things will be done. Tacit supervision does not put goals and expectations into a specific covenant. If a covenant exists, it covers only "safe" areas, ignoring the hidden agenda. Since mission personnel are never sure of boundaries, they may be surprised by reprimands any time.

Tacit supervision creates problems for everyone and, eventually, for the supervisor. Usually fear and mistrust are behind tacit supervision since the supervisor trusts neither himself nor herself, the mission personnel or the system.

METHODS OF SUPERVISION

There are three easily identifiable methods of supervision described in this book: administration, reward and supportive. A supervisor may use multiple methods or depend primarily on one method.

Supervision by Administration

Supervision by administration is supervising by administrative procedures, such as personnel policy, calendar schedules, work guidelines and task goals. Everything is done in an impersonal manner so that mission personnel interact with policy rather than with the supervisor. Reviewing the work of persons using this method, observers have found that personhood issues are incidental or not attended. While this is a traditional method of supervision in the corporate world, it fails to account for the Christian presupposition that people count.

Reward Supervision

This method of supervision is the old carrot-and-stick approach. The reward may be financial or psychological stroking. For example, at the annual performance review, personnel learn whether the organization will fund their program the following year or whether they receive an increase or decrease in program funds or salary. This method tends to be impersonal. Theoretically the reward method of supervision can emphasize personhood issues; however, observation shows that it is a way to avoid dealing with personhood. Also, religious groups seldom have adequate resources to reward properly.

Supportive Supervision

The supportive supervisor builds a support system around the mission personnel that serves them during normal and critical times. This direct, personal approach may use administrative methods and provide rewards, but the focus is supporting the mission personnel systemically and personally.

STAGES OF SUPERVISION

Supervision is development, which means it goes through stages. The supervisor who is aware and uses these stages helps make the experience more beneficial. Ignoring the stages often creates confusion and problems that are difficult to identify. Just as travelers need road maps to guide them from one point to another, a knowledge of stages of supervision can help the supervisor. The supervisor who remembers the axiom, "structure binds anxiety," can face the new supervision role with confidence.   Supervisors who begin their role aware of the stages will have a structure that can lead to a rewarding relationship. Little or no structure opens the way for capriciousness. On the other hand, the structure can be so cumbersome that people become preoccupied with the mechanics.

There are three stages during the supervision pilgrimage: initiating, structure and termination. The supervisor, aware of these stages, enhances the supervision experience.

The Initiating Stage

This is the "get-acquainted" stage. The supervisor acquaints mission personnel with structure, expectations, taboos and fellow workers.   This may be a brief period when the new person is not a novice in the work and there is little cultural dissonance. However, there are circumstances when this can be an extended period. A Foreign Mission Board executive wrote:

> A new arrival is reduced to a state of almost total dependence (arriving) where English is little used. They cannot read the street signs, or names of buildings, or directions on appliances. The first stages to adjusting to living outside of a familiar environment can be more stressful than anything they have encountered up to this point in their lives.

Under these conditions, the supervisor can count on a long initiating stage.

Supervisors need to take initiative in sharing their pilgrimages appropriately. While the name, age and serial number approach expresses interest only in mechanics, legalities or organization, the mission personnel may not be ready to hear the most intimate details of the supervisor's life and experiences.   Intimacy not earned creates barriers. When mission personnel see both commonalities and differences between themselves and their supervisor, it helps them identify with the experiences and struggles of the supervisor.

A good supervisor can help mission personnel understand the systems and expectations within which they will be working.

During this "get-acquainted stage," supervisors and mission personnel can relate their expectations. This stage is the time to formalize these expectations and develop the covenant.

During this stage, the wise supervisor will need to introduce mission personnel to the official and informal structures. If a mission person works in a ghetto, the supervisor may discuss practical things like walking alone on the street at night. There may be taboos that a new person in a foreign country may need to know. If work is in a mission center or a congregation, the supervisor may say, "Don't disturb Aunt Suzie's picture in the church foyer or move the ugly vase off the communion table." Supervisors can help by pointing out the "land mines" located in the informal structures.

Ritualizing the presence and responsibility of the new person shows that something new is happening. Something deep within the human mind calls for ritualizations of beginnings and endings. Not many ministers want couples to live together without the ritualization of the beginning of their relationship in a marriage ceremony. A young couple may argue that saying a few words over them does not make things any different, but the minister usually believes that the initiating rite of a marriage ceremony is important. A ritual at the beginning of a new supervision relationship provides the first step toward becoming a team.

When the supervision setting is a congregation, the supervisor may schedule an initiating rite for the first Sunday worship service attended by the new worker. The supervisor can place a notice in a bulletin (if there is one), formally introduce the person and explain his or her role and responsibilities. Some congregations will appreciate a litany of dedication where the supervisor, mission personnel and congregation state their commitment to a partnership in the Lord's work. Where the new person will serve as a mission pastor and the supervisor is a denominational executive (such as a director of missions), the pastor may invite the denominational executive to participate.

The Southern Baptist mission boards have commissioning services for new appointees. The field where the appointees serve can hold a similar rite of initiation.

The Structural or Task Stage

This is the stage of routine supervision where the supervision relationship is consciously and formally structured. It is the stage when the mission personnel carry out their primary work. During the regular supervision conferences, the mission personnel bring appropriate reports and give accountability according to the covenant. This is the stage in which the supervisor looks for growth in the mission personnel.

The axiom applicable to this stage is: "Move from high structure to lower structure." When you move from high to low structure, you have the comfort of high structure at the beginning and affirm the person as you move to lower structure. You can decrease the frequency of the supervision conferences when the relationship and work go well. The accountability can become less stringent. If you begin with low structure and have to move to higher structure, you create anxiety and resentment.

Although final evaluation comes later, evaluation should be continuous. Mission personnel can know as they go along that they are fulfilling their covenant and expectations when the supervisor affirms them throughout this stage. Continuing evaluation leads to opportunities to renegotiate the covenant when new areas of attention arise during this stage.

The task stage is the longest period of the three. It is the time for effective and productive work and personhood growth.

The Termination Stage

It is axiomatic that we begin to die the moment we are born. Termination begins on the first day of the relationship. The termination period is a specific time when the supervisor and mission personnel consciously bring the relationship to a close. Termination is most productive when they plan transition in the ministry once the personnel have left and examine the future role of the mission personnel. It may be a time to redefine roles; the mission personnel may be moving to a different field of service or ending a relationship with the mission board, or developing a new covenant.

Psychologically it is important to draw a relationship and

work to a close. A young college student spent summer doing mission work at an inner city center in a distant state. When she met her parents at the airport upon returning home, she hugged her father and sobbed, "He didn't even tell me good-bye." The center director had left Friday as though it were another day and did not acknowledge that this was the mission volunteer's last day. Someone else had taken her to the airport. There had been no closure. The next summer the college student took a week's vacation from her summer job and returned to the center for the children's camp. It was her way of bringing closure to her mission experience.

Mission personnel may need to examine the future relationships with the supervisor as the formal, covenanted relationship ends. The supervisor may make a conscious decision that he or she will no longer function as the person's supervisor although continuing to relate in another capacity. Friendship may continue beyond the supervision relationship but redefine the relationship. The termination stage can clarify a future relationship and avoid unresolved feelings.

Termination rites are as important as initiation rites. These rites signal the end of the covenant of accountability and of the previous relationship. Termination rites are especially important when the mission personnel continues at the mission site beyond the mission term. A mission board appointed a young man for a two-year assignment working at a church with troubled youth. After the two years, the young man remained in the city to work on a master's degree. He continued to work in the church. Conflict occurred with the arrival of a new worker. The former mission appointee never accepted his new role and the congregation never transferred allegiance. Termination rites would have signaled a new relationship to both the congregation and the mission personnel.

Recently a foreign missionary told me that a colleague was nearing retirement but was not leaving the area where he had spent most of his adult life. The missionary had deep investments in the people and the region. Other foreign missionaries face separation from fellow missionaries with whom they have worked closely and significant work which they have to leave. Termination is going to happen, and a good termination stage will help provide good closure.

STATES OF SUPERVISION

"Stage" is one lens to look through to examine supervision. Another lens is the "state" of supervision. The states of supervision describe the quality of the working relationship between the supervisor and mission personnel. People in working relationships pass through four states in the following order; structure, cooperation, fellowship and partnership (see chart on page 50). [1] They cannot decide arbitrarily to start in one of the states but begin in the first state—the structure state. A person cannot set dates to be at any of the states but has to earn movement from one state to the other. An alert supervisor can recognize the move from one state to another.

The states are not absolute. Their boundaries are "fuzzy" enough that people may revert (consciously or unconsciously) back to a former state. People who are aware of the states may move through them more quickly and deliberately than if they were not aware.

The states are bounded by task and personhood. For example, in state three, the fellowship state, supervision focuses on personhood. In this state, personhood, not tasks, is the primary concern, although tasks get done.

Many supervision relationships stop permanently in one of the first three states. People may find a particular state productive and refuse to change patterns, or they may find one especially comfortable. Each state reflects the experience, history and natural inclination of the supervisor. Problems may develop when people have idealized concepts of relationships coming out of their family background or earlier positions. They may think that proper relationships are non-egalitarian. However, since people are held accountable, there is no complete non-egalitarianism. Some may have experienced supervision only as autocratic and assume that is the mark of supervision.

---

[1]See Doran C. McCarty, *Supervising Ministry Students* (Atlanta: Home Mission Board, SBC, 1978), p. 66.

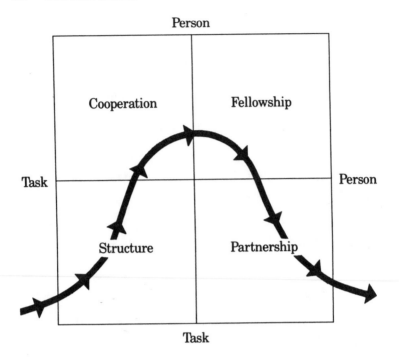

The Structure State

This is a task/task state. Early in the relationship, the supervisor has little information or observation to deal with personhood issues. This state has high structure characterized by the supervisor outlining responsibilities, resources and methods. It is a state in which the supervisor "tells" personnel about the tasks and the structures. When this state is productive, it is tempting to stay in it. However, if the missionary is to mature in the ministry and shows initiative, the supervisor has to move out of the structure state. While this state is good for a beginning, the supervisor will push the relationship on when the missionary is capable of growth and responsibility.

The Cooperation State

This is a task/personhood state. The supervisor changes from "telling" to "asking" in the cooperation state. Here the supervisor begins to take the personhood of the missionary into consideration. By this time, the missionary has learned about the structure and responsibilities and has shown commitment to the Lord and the work. The missionary is ready to take more direct responsibility. The supervisor has also learned more about the missionary. Through observations, the covenant and the supervision conferences, the supervisor can deal with more personhood issues.

The Fellowship State

This state is personhood/personhood. Leaving the cooperation state may be difficult because the fellowship state is person-oriented with a tendency toward intimacy, and intimacy can be threatening. The fellowship state may also be the idealized state that a supervisor envisions about any relationship. This state is a productive time for planning and achieving, not simply a time to enjoy each other.

The Partnership State

The partnership state is another personhood/tasks state. This is not a regression to the previous task/personhood state. Because personhood is highlighted in the fellowship state, there is increased respect for and trust of the person entering the partnership state. In the partnership state, the supervisor makes the missionary a partner in the project, not simply someone who cooperates in the work. This means that the missionary has a voice in decisions and greater ownership of plans and actions. Sometimes supervisors in the fellowship state fear moving into the partnership state because they must give away some control.

When you begin with a new missionary, start in the structure state with the highest structure you will ever need. If you have had a previous relationship with the person, you can maintain that relationship if you define your supervision role carefully.

Problems develop when a supervisor has several mission personnel for whom he or she is responsible. Because of differences in tenure, experience, training and maturity, they may move through states at varying paces. A new person may feel that the supervisor is playing favorites unless the supervisor explains about states.

A change of supervisors creates a new scenario and brings a new relationship. The Foreign Mission Board assigned a new couple to work under the supervision of a veteran missionary. However, the supervisor's furlough came within a year after the assignment. Area staff realized that there would be changes and planned for special arrangements for the new missionaries. While this probably hastened moving into the cooperation state, it also meant that they had to address some issues of the structure state.

A crisis may require moving back into an earlier state, even the structure state. When the crisis is over, the relationship may return to its previous state.

SYSTEMS AND SUPERVISION

The western part of the United States contains rich mineral deposits. A company wanted to mine high quality coal in a western state. The company foresaw great profit and the state governor saw an opportunity to bring jobs into a job-poor area. The terrain was suitable for the operation of heavy equipment and a railroad spur. Many unemployed or under-employed persons could work in the coal mines.

One major obstacle existed. The land belonged to a Native American tribe that had used the land for centuries for sacred ceremonies. Because of sacred traditions, they did not want to give up the land despite the economic factors. Without success, company officials tried to convince the tribe of advantages the mining would provide. The company even offered to build historical monuments and provide another place for ceremonial exercises, but anywhere else would not be the sacred ceremonial grounds.

Several systems are involved in this story about the mining company and the Native American community. The systems are generally unrelated. The mining company is a Midwestern corporation with no experience of mining in the West. The two systems may be generally compatible, both living and supporting national interests, but in this situation, they are incompatible.

As individuals, employees of the mining company and members of the Native American community could have served on the same Navy ship or attended the same college. But they are not merely individuals; they are also part of larger systems. When they function in those systems, they become incompatible. They may bring the issue before the Bureau of Indian Affairs (another system), a department of the state government that controls mining operations (still another system), or eventually before a court of law, introducing yet another system.

A system is a person, persons or entity needs, goals, boundaries and understandings. A corporate entity is a system consisting perhaps of officers such as board of directors, president, vice president, treasurer, several managers, laborers, properties and traditions. A person is a system formed by diverse experiences, a unique history, and several goals and is thus subject to many demands.

An effective supervisor will not ignore systems but learn to recognize them. A seminary graduate took a pastorate in a small county seat town. When asked why he had sought this appointment, he answered that this would be a good place to learn how to identify power structures and systems and then he could serve effectively anywhere. His next pastorate was in a city in the deep South during racial turmoil. Because he had learned about systems, he mobilized the systems in his church and the city to deal with the racial injustices in the community. A supervisor who is not effective in recognizing systems will likely destruct by crashing into systems instead of finding ways to use them.

Each system relates to other systems. A family illustrates this. John Doe comes from one family or system. Mary Doe comes from another. These systems impinge upon the new family created by the couple's marriage. John is also a part of several other systems. He works for an automobile manufacturer. He belongs to the Kiwanis Club, the Methodist church and the Democratic Party. His wife works at a department store, is a member of a Baptist church and a secretary to the P.T.A.. Their son, Jim, attends a junior high school and plays football for a little league team. Their daughter, Jane, attends an elementary school, plays in the orchestra and is a Girl Scout. Other systems involving this family may include labor unions, banks they do business with, the credit cards they hold and their individual circle of friends. Each family member relates to the other members' systems.

What happens when Jim has a little league football game on the same Saturday that John must work on the union contract negotiating team? What happens when John's union opposes the Democratic candidate for Congress? Or where do the children attend church? Do they attend John's Methodist church or Mary's Baptist church?

Systems overlap, but they are not identical. For example, if a congregation has twenty Sunday School classes, there is a great deal of overlapping. Classes may obtain Sunday School literature from the same publisher and meet simultaneously but not be identical. The King's Daughters may sing "The Old Rugged Cross" slowly and sentimentally while the youth class sings a gospel rock musical accompanied by a cassette tape played over four amplifiers. Two Baptist congregations may belong to the same convention and send their money to the same mission board, but they are not identical. They are two different systems operating within a third.

System Boundaries

Each system has its own components and boundaries. The boundaries of the system of the United States are the fifty states, their territories, their embassies and citizens. The congregation's boundaries are its property and its members. Boundaries fluctuate. For example, the family system may include parents and children and, at other times, grandparents and other relatives. Boundaries are not only physical territories but psychological territories. Any man who recalls his childhood remembers fights started not only when struck physically but also when taunted by words.

System Needs

Another system component is need. Needs are required to maintain a system. Human needs can be defined as the basic drives (hunger, thirst, sex, etc.). Like humans, organizations have needs to be satisfied. A system's basic need is to continue. People within a system may take criticism as a threat to the existence of the system upon which they depend.

System Goals

Systems also have goals. A congregation goal may be to build a sanctuary. A business goal may be to open a store in a new shopping mall. A family's goal may be to own a house, to finance a son's education or to pay their debts. If you want to work with a system, you have to understand its goals.

Systems' Self-understanding

Understanding and self-identity are vital to the system. A system may understand itself to be a profit-making or a not-for-profit institution. A church may understand itself to be liberal or conservative. The denomination may perceive itself as missionary or orthodox. Systems may see themselves as helpful, impoverished, wealthy, necessary, powerful or weak. Others may see them differently, but comprehending and working successfully with a system means knowing how the system understands itself.

System Accountability

Many different forms of accountability exist, and every system has some form. A person who works within a system can expect the system to demand accountability.

Systems' Development

Systems go through developmental stages. They grow in numbers and tradition, creating changes. When there are only four or five associates, a supervisor can visit all quite often. When the system grows to fifty associates, the supervisor has to change the system. The original four or five might not understand that the system has reached a new stage and not understand the supervisor's new way of functioning.

The Interrelatedness of Systems

When you want to work with a system, it is important to understand system components. Two systems may not have identical goals but, to work together, they need compatible goals. Systems work together because they honor and share each other's boundaries and conceptions. Each system must meet some needs of the other systems.

A congregation wanted to start a chapel in a new subdivision at the edge of town. The congregation paid a substantial price for three acres of land, engaged an architect and developed plans, arranged financing and surveyed the community for prospects for the new mission. When they applied for a building permit, it was denied. The area was zoned for single family, detached residences only. The sponsoring congregation experienced a great deal of anger and frustration. They needed to establish a new chapel while the city needed to provide a stable community with safe public services. The two systems conflicted because they had differing needs and goals. Each system had its own components and was insensitive to the needs of the other system.

Foreign missionaries often find frustrations with regulations which foreign nations place on them. However, they have to find a way to work with the systems of the country if they wish to be guests in the country.

Imperfect Systems

All systems have imperfections. Imperfect systems may have imperfect goals. They may have erroneous understandings about themselves or others. They may also have misconceptions about how things are done. Systems are imperfect because imperfect people are in systems. People are touched by original sin; systems are also victims of corporate sin.

It is tempting to shun relationships with imperfect systems or to withdraw when discovering their imperfections. This, however, is no more reasonable than withdrawing from imperfect people. Counselors do not recommend that mates leave spouses when they discover imperfection. After all, marriages made of imperfect people can function in a positive and affirming way. Systems, too, can benefit from one another despite imperfections.

Systems and Symbiotic Relationships

Systems may develop a symbiotic relationship in which two people (or systems) serve a positive function for one another. An interesting illustration of this is the relationship of the shark and the pilot fish. The shark, a carnivorous fish, looks for smaller victims to attack and eat. Yet it allows pilot fish to nibble away parasites or even enter the shark's mouth to clean out remnants of food collected around its teeth. In this symbiotic relationship the pilot fish gives the shark a worthwhile service while receiving a good meal from the shark in return. Systems develop similar symbiotic relationships with one another. Differences in goals, needs and understandings may exist between two systems, but they can serve each other symbiotically.

A Baptist congregation appealed to the local Baptist association for help in establishing a mission in a nearby town. Since the association lacked funds, the director of missions appealed to the state Baptist convention for help. The sponsoring congregation, the association, the state convention and the Home Mission Board agreed to work together on the project. The Home Mission Board sent a team during the summer to make surveys and lay groundwork. The sponsoring congregation's pastor and the director of missions supervised the project. The state convention provided funds to purchase a site; in cooperation with the Home Mission Board it provided a salary supplement for a mission pastor.

Several systems in a symbiotic relationship helped to create a mission congregation. Each entity (the sponsoring congregation, the association, the state convention and the Home Mission Board) participated to fulfill its tasks while helping the other systems do the same. Each had limiting boundaries and, within this symbiotic relationship, each system had to develop self-imposed boundaries. Yet each system received benefit enough so each was willing to accept the self-imposed limitations and be part of the systems network.

You can usually work with systems when you understand the way they work and provided they do not violate your system. When someone tries to circumvent the system, problems usually develop. A foreign missionary requested assistance directly rather than going through the usual system. When the person arrived to assist, he was immediately told that the situation in the country was too dangerous and that he would have to go to another country, which he did. Soon the missionary in that country reported that the person was unacceptable. When the supervisors, who were responsible for the area, investigated, they transferred the new missionary to another assignment and his work went well. Not working within the system is a red flag.

Inadequate Systems

When there is an inadequate system for proper supervision, the supervisor may have to create an adequate local system to meet the situation. The covenant becomes the centerpiece since it provides the guidelines for the supervision relationship. While a person can lobby with mission groups for a better supervision system, there may be a period before an adequate system is in place. This is a challenge to the supervisor to work within that system but provide the support the missionary needs.

Systems may seem to impede work at times, but they are always present and usually are necessary to get work done.

Changing Systems

Persons entering a system often see its imperfections and inadequacies and want to change the system. A wise leader will want to review a system periodically to learn how to improve the system. Often an outside consultant is helpful in reviewing the system. It may be helpful to do this before a new person joins the system to review the need to change roles.

There is a price to pay for changing a system. Personnel may be uncomfortable with systemic changes since they are accustomed to their roles in the present system. There may be fear of loss of favorite tasks or position or prestige. Changing systems may disrupt the work flow for a time. Change may energize or enervate personnel.

A new president took over a company and made significant changes. They were hardly in place until he made more changes. He repeated this several times. When an associate asked why he kept making changes, he responded that each time changes were made, people became more energetic. However, if changes happen in an atmosphere of mistrust, the opposite can happen and new energy can become resentment.

A person who wants to make changes will likely face opposition and resistance. The old is comfortable. If the person desiring change is new, others will resist (even if they see the wisdom of the change) because the new person has not "paid his dues." This is especially true when the changes are to copy ways other agencies do their work. A new church planter in the North created problems for himself when he tried to get local denominational people to do things "the way they do in Texas." It was not long until he was back in Texas. Persons wanting to make changes in systems will learn that they have to pay the price for change.

Foreign missionaries have reported about new missionaries coming to a country for the first time and immediately trying to begin significant change in goals or operation of the mission. The new missionaries are often surprised by the reaction of veteran missionaries. The veteran missionaries have "paid their dues" and the new missionary has not. The new missionary may pay the price of feeling ostracized and rejected when his or her new ideas are not accepted.

CHAPTER 6

METHODS OF SUPERVISION

Supervision, as other disciplines, has methods that have proved effective in advancing the work of the discipline. Two of these methods for supervision are developing the covenant and conducting supervisory conferences.

DEVELOPING THE COVENANT

Covenants are instruments to guide and clarify relationships, roles and responsibilities between persons. A covenant states what people expect and the nature of the rewards. Synonyms for covenant are contract, agreement, pact and treaty. I use the word "covenant" because of its biblical heritage. Covenant is the most accurate translation of the Latin term transliterated "testament." God made a covenant with Abraham, and Jeremiah spoke of a new covenant in the heart. Jesus symbolized His covenant with the bread and wine at the Last Supper. Covenants have a long and rich religious history.

It is important for covenanting parties to write out the covenant rather than depend on an oral agreement. The written covenant provides a reminder and helps supervisors evaluate situations and persons more precisely. A good supervisor will review the covenant periodically in order to assure that the mission personnel are progressing. (See pages 61 and 62 for a good example of a written covenant.)

SAMPLE COVENANT

Covenant Dates: 9/10/96 through 9/10/97.

Job Title: Area Consultant.

Scheduled Supervisory Session: Tuesday, 10:00 A.M.

Weekly Schedule: Be flexible with consultant, depending on area, number of churches, and availability.

Covenant Goals:

Need: To inform churches in our area concerning mission opportunities through volunteer ministries.
Goal: To contact twenty-five churches in our area concerning volunteer opportunities by 9/10/97.
Activities: (1) Call and write every pastor and missions education leader in the association, (2) set up appointments to meet personally with church leaders; (3) prepare materials and send to each mission leader, etc.

Need: To develop my spiritual life.
Goal: To spend twenty minutes each day toward developing my devotional life for duration of covenant period.
Activities: (1) Secure appropriate time, (2) discover appropriate material to study; (3) secure a place for quiet time.

Need: To identify needs that could be serviced by volunteers.
Goal: Process the appropriate request form for each justifiable need.
Activities: (1) Visit with director of missions to determine assoc iational needs; (2) visit with pastors and missions development leaders to determine local church needs; (3) study demographic materials to know the area and potential needs.

Need: To learn to use a personal computer.
Goal: Take one complete introduction-to-the-computer course from

college or business school.

Activities: (1) Discover what kind of course work is available in my
area; (2) secure reading materials on basic computer skills; (3)
secure the use of a computer for learning and practice.

Evaluation: The supervisor will provide a written and oral evaluation every
six months. The supervisor will provide a written and oral self-
evaluation every six months. Criteria for evaluation will be the
written goals of the covenant.

The covenant is an instrument for defining accountability.
Systems necessitate accountability. When someone sends money
to another person, a covenant outlines the accountability. For
example, the Southern Baptist Convention funds the mission
boards and holds the boards accountable through a set of
program statements.

The Home Mission Board develops a (written) "cooperative
agreement" with each state Baptist convention spelling out the
terms of their cooperation in mission work. For example,
mission personnel are jointly appointed by the Home Mission
Board and the state Baptist convention. The Home Mission
Board holds the state Baptist convention accountable for Home
Mission Board funds used in mission work as agreed upon by
the two agencies. The state Baptist convention may turn to
associational directors of missions or others for supervision of
the mission personnel. The covenant also provides limitations
of accountability. If a mission agency appointment is to one
department, he or she is not accountable for the work of other
departments.

Often two agreements are required; one between the mission
board and congregation and another between the supervisor and
the mission personnel. The covenant between the mission board
and the congregation spells out the broad parameters and goals
for the work. The covenant between the supervisor and mission
personnel is under the umbrella of the covenant between the
mission board and the congregation, but it delineates goals and
actions of mission personnel. The covenant between the supervisor and mission personnel outlines areas of personal growth

for the mission personnel.   Personal growth is not contrary to the mission agency goals, but facilitates all phases of work.

A good covenant with mission personnel will cover task and personhood issues. As goals are written, it will be useful to name each goal as to whether it is task or personhood. The supervisor should approve a covenant only when there are adequate personhood goals. During a covenant review, the personhood goals should receive full attention.

A Job Description and the Covenant

The job description and covenant are two separate items. The job description delineates the responsibilities of a position. This is usually developed before offering a person a position. It is task oriented. It doesn't matter who takes the job; the job description is the same. It remains the same each year.

The covenant sets goals that will fulfill the job description. Each person brings skills and interests that can be addressed in the covenant but not the job description. Above all, the covenant deals with personhood issues while the job description does not.

Types of Covenants

Formal covenants.   The formal covenant is intentional, written and in technical language.   The best example is a document which an attorney draws up for a court.   Formal covenants spell out the conditions to which each part of the system agrees. Few covenants between supervisors and mission personnel will be formal.

Informal covenants. Informal covenants are intentional and sometimes written, but they are never in technical language. Informal covenants are made all the time, such as a luncheon appointment. Every day we depend on informal covenants to carry out our ministry functions and our personal lives.

Tacit covenants.   Tacit covenants are those with hidden aspects or motives. While we rarely admit the hidden issues in a tacit covenant, both parties are usually aware of them. The tacit covenant may exist alongside a "real" covenant, and the parties agree to act according to the tacit covenant. Supervisors who operate from tacit covenants can hold others accountable as they wish. Victims of a tacit covenant never know when they will be held accountable. They often become the "fall guys." Part of the covenanting process should be to flush out all possible tacit aspects so that the covenant is a clear document.

Questions about the Covenant

Before the supervisor and the mission personnel begin to develop the covenant, there are questions they should ask. Answers offer resources to create a good covenant.

What do the systems require? All systems (e.g., mission board, congregation, etc.) have requirements such as reporting and specific activities. The covenant that ignores system requirements is defective and may create problems.

What are the goals? Goals are the heart of any covenant. The supervisor and mission personnel should clearly identify the goals to be accomplished in both mission work and personal growth.

What are the strengths of the mission personnel? Each person involved in missions has his or her own unique strengths. Supervisors can help mission personnel to articulate these strengths and tie them to appropriate goals. Some strengths are in varying stages of growth and may be latent within mission personnel. The supervisor may assist further development of individual abilities so the person is able to function adequately if not expertly.

What are available resources? Resources within the local ministry situation, the denomination, various secular agencies or in literature facilitate nearly every task. People serving in underdeveloped countries may have to re-think what resources will suffice.

What procedures will be followed? When the supervisor and mission personnel enter the covenant, they should consider procedures developed by mission boards or congregations. Local or state agencies may shape the procedures, and these need to be taken into account in the covenant. In foreign countries missionaries reside at the pleasure of the national government.

What is the process of renegotiation? A covenant should contain a time and process for renegotiation.

What is the evaluation process? Both the supervisor and mission personnel profit from evaluation. An evaluation process should be established early in the relationship.

What about approval? The covenant must be approved by all the parties involved. Mission systems may have an approval process to be followed.

The Process of Covenant Making

Many different processes work. Here is one way of developing a covenant which, when followed faithfully, can lead to a covenant which will guide the relationships, roles and responsibilities.

1. Determine expectations and needs. I believe that it is wise to begin with needs even if they seem to be redundant in the process. Too many people look at what is succeeding elsewhere and set their goals. Their place of service may have different needs.

Expectations and needs may be two different things. Supervisors may have different expectations than mission personnel. This is especially true for new people arriving on a mission field. The mission agency may have a set of expectations as well as the local constituency. Personhood needs should not be overlooked.

2. Determine the goal. Goals are statements of desired outcome. They should relate to the identified needs. Goals should be specific, measurable, practical and attainable.

3. Plan the actions. The work accomplished in the previous steps will fail if actions fail to fulfill expectations and needs and to meet the goals. Actions involve specific programs to meet the goals. Actions should have a set time line to assist accountability. It takes several actions to reach one goal.

4. Develop an evaluation system. You evaluate goals, not actions. Evaluation provides "mile posts" so mission personnel and supervisors can assess whether or not the goals are being met.   The times, process and criteria for evaluation should be stated in the covenant. This should include terms of accountability. (The form of accountability may be written or oral or a combination.) Task goals are usually easier to evaluate because they can be quantified. Personhood goals are often subjective enough that evaluation depends upon the observation of observers.   Subjective evaluation is not bad because lay persons subjectively evaluate ministers all the time (although they may never report their evaluations to the minister).

There should be routine evaluation.   The supervisor should give some evaluation at the end of each conference with the mission personnel. A structured evaluation during the year will give mission personnel an opportunity to make "mid-course corrections."   A final evaluation will summarize the covenant period. The time and form of the mid-course and final evaluations will be described in the covenant.

Evaluation should be based on the task and personal goals in the covenant.   The covenant is important to indicate areas of examination but also the limits of examination.

The evaluation session format follows a specific structure. The mission personnel will profit from a written self-evaluation of their fulfillment of the covenant goals. If they turn this in to the supervisor before final evaluation, the supervisor will have that data as part of the evaluation.

When the supervisor presents an evaluation, the mission personnel should have an opportunity to respond. The supervisor should not attempt to defend his or her evaluation or introduce new material. However, it is possible that the supervisor will gain new insight from the mission personnel's response, and, if this significantly changes the supervisor's evaluation, the supervisor should relate it to the mission personnel. Whenever possible, the format of the evaluation should end with the mission personnel's response to the supervisor.

To prepare for the evaluation, supervisors may develop a grid for separating out the patterns of functions of mission personnel. Without a grid, areas for evaluation may not appear dramatically and escape the supervisor's attention. Supervisors can individualize general grid systems that exist for ministers system according to the particular ministry situation. This may include facility in foreign language, ability to lead worship services, expertise in stewardship or financial matters, ability to lead organizations, ability to motivate people and adjusting to cultural situations.

One goal in evaluation is to fulfill the requirements of the systems involved. Evaluation also functions to monitor growth and demonstrate adequate functioning of the mission personnel. Evaluation provides opportunity for the support of mission personnel.

Special Covenant Considerations

There is no way to anticipate all the problems that might be addressed in a covenant. However, some consideration about time, work and behavior will help.

What kind of time expectations do you have? Yours may be different from the person coming to work with you. A youth team came to New York City to "do ministry." Their contact person in New York City promised a church that the youth team would help them from 9:00 until 4:00 each day in Vacation Bible Schools and backyard Bible studies. After the first day, the youth complained to their youth minister because they had planned to spend afternoons being tourists. On Thursday they also had a day trip planned.

You may work until a job is accomplished and assume that others work the same way. The person coming to work with you has always had an 8:00 to 4:00 job and assumes everyone works off the union shop model. The type and intensity of the work should be addressed in the covenant. The missionary may not see "paper work" as important even though the system requires it.

Behaviors are difficult to put in the covenant unless there has been a previous problem with another person or the cultural patterns demand it. My wife and I took a team of students to Belize so they could test out their desire to become foreign missionaries. Otis Brady, the missionary in Belize City, wrote to the team before we left the states, outlining certain behaviors that would not be acceptable in that culture. We could live by them or stay home.

CONDUCTING THE
SUPERVISORY CONFERENCE

The supervisory conference is the heart of supervision. Conferences should be scheduled regularly. The supervisor needs an agenda to follow, especially during the first year. Detailed agenda may be determined in response to the situations and to insight into the mission personnel's work.

The supervisory conference is a specific time when the supervisor and personnel meet to deal with agenda. It is not a quick conversation at a happenstance meeting in the hallway nor "lunch together." It is a formal, structured time where the supervisor gives the personnel his or her full attention. Interruptions, such as phone calls, are not allowed. The supervisor's time belongs to the supervisee. The supervisory conference is not a staff meeting. The staff meeting includes the whole staff to care for task issues relating to everyone. The supervisory conference is the supervisor's time with one person where they can deal with that one person's task progress and personhood issues.

Times of Supervisory Conferences

The time frame for supervision gives a clue to the supervisor's style of supervision. When supervisory conferences are held largely determine their effectiveness. Below are some observations about various supervisory conference times.

1. Routine supervisory conferences. Supervisors schedule routine supervisory conferences regularly. When possible, they are scheduled at the same time and day each period (weekly, biweekly, etc.). This helps to create a disciplined approach to supervision. Both parties know the time and can prepare. This allows specific times to raise questions, express opinions and receive information and thus it avoids unnecessary anxiety. The supervisor is able to monitor the plans and work of the mission personnel regularly.

The routine supervisory conference structures the relationship to enhance the partnership of the supervisor and personnel. It is like an army platoon marching in cadence so that each step becomes "second nature."

When the supervisory conference is routine, it takes less time. Personnel know that they will have time with the supervisor and can hold agenda until they meet rather than constantly interrupting the supervisor at other times.

2. Occasional supervisory conferences.   The occasional supervisory conference is where the supervisor calls a conference from time to time but holds no regular conferences. Occasional supervisory conferences usually take place when the supervisor has an agenda for the mission personnel. This may be a request for something to be done or it may involve checking out a problem. Occasional supervisory conferences create anxiety. Personnel assume something is wrong when the supervisor calls a conference. The result can be defensiveness and resistance. Occasional conferences make it difficult for the personnel who attend to be prepared for what the supervisor wants to discuss.

3. Seasonal supervisory conferences.   There are certain tasks that have to be done during the year. Reports have to be submitted to mission agencies, budgets have to be prepared and personnel nominations have to be made. When the supervisor recognizes these special tasks need to be performed, he or she may set a supervisory conference. Seasonal supervision is directed toward task issues so that personhood issues are not attended.

4. Project supervisory conferences.   The supervisor may call on mission personnel to do special projects. Often the supervisor does not give attention to the mission personnel's routine work and personhood during project supervision but only deals with a special project.

5. Crisis supervisory conferences.   Many supervisors function on a crisis basis. It is often expressed this way by the supervisor: "Whenever you have a problem, come to me." supervisors should always be open to crisis situations, but supervisory conferences only at times of crises reinforces a negative attitude about the supervisor. For attention, suffering mission personnel may even create a crisis.   Typically, the monkey of the crisis is put on the supervisor's back and before he or she can deal with it, there is a call for another crisis conference (with another monkey for the supervisor's back).

The best alternative for supervisory conferences is the routine conference. It provides disciplined supervision and builds confidence in the supervisor. It also signals to mission personnel that they are worthwhile since the supervisor sets specific time for them alone.

The Structure of the Supervisory Conference [1]

I have asked persons attending seminars to do a supervisory conference exercise. Afterwards I ask whether they felt more comfortable in the supervisor role or the participant role. Most feel the greatest anxiety in the supervisor role. When you are the supervisor, you determine agenda and direct the discussion. If you are uncertain how you should function, you become anxious. The axiom is: "Structure binds anxiety." The supervisor who follows the suggested structure will have lessened anxiety. There may be anxiety over the subject matter you have to discuss, but you will not have anxiety over the process. With experience the process will become second nature to you and you won't have to concentrate on the process.

1. Pre-conference preparation. Good supervisors review notes made on previous meetings, set goals for the supervisory conference, make and prioritize the agenda. Without a prioritized agenda, the supervisor may not be able to meet the information needs of a system or address critical agenda issues of mission personnel.

First of all, review your notes from the last meeting. See if

---

[1] Dr. James Goodson, state mission director, Florida Baptist Convention, has developed a notebook for supervision, and he keeps one on each of his supervisees. He retires the notebook at the end of each year and begins a new one. There are four parts to the notebook. The first section is for objectives, goals, and action plans. The second section is for copies of memos sent to and received from the supervisee. The third section is made up of supervision sheets for each month, indicating agenda and results of each supervisory conference. The fourth section is for travel reports (expenses and itinerary).

there are some issues you agreed to address in the upcoming conference. Perhaps you promised to bring information to the meeting. You need to review your notes from the past several months at least quarterly. This gives you an overview to see patterns in the person with whom you are working. The patterns are more important than a single incident.

Make a list of possible agenda items. While you may find agenda items in the notes on your previous conference, you will want to look ahead to future events and plans. Since you will probably have more items on the agenda than you can cover, you need to set priorities. Priorities are usually based on time limits and importance. When you have the conference, other issues of importance may arise. It is important to have your priorities listed so they can be addressed separately from other agenda items.

2. The supervisory conference. A profitable way to begin the supervisory conference is with a "ritual of mutuality" where the two of you briefly exchange "small talk." In American culture you cannot productively plunge into agenda without some ritual of mutuality. Yet if this discussion is lengthy, either the supervisor or the mission personnel may be trying to avoid a situation or agenda issues. The most natural rituals of mutuality are discussions about the weather, sports or major news stories.

The good supervisor reviews the agenda, providing opportunities for mission personnel to place issues on the agenda and to negotiate priorities. This is your covenant for the supervisory conference.

The mission personnel will want to review activities since the last supervisory conference and preview work plans between this conference and the next. Special projects will need to be reviewed. The supervisor may set times to observe mission personnel on the job. A supervisor may review task reports submitted by mission personnel or others. Written reports create a greater sense of accountability and cause mission personnel to reflect on their ministries. Written reports may cut down the possibilities of game-playing and misinterpretation.

There are a number of ways that a person can document accounts of his or her ministry, including verbatims, process notes, case studies and critical incidents. If the ministry action contact is a single incident, the best form will include three parts: the introduction detailing the background material (situation, incident and people) involved; an account of the conversation; and third, summary of the main issues, examined theologically, psychologically and sociologically.

Mission personnel may keep a ministry journal. It provides a good record of plans and actions. Ministry journals reveal the mission personnel's pattern of functioning. The ministry journal records time and schedule study. Through journal keeping, ministers, who often reach the end of the day feeling that they have not accomplished enough, take time to reflect upon their achievements. A good ministry journal contains several sections.

The first part records daily plans, while the second accounts for the day in a series of 15-minute segments. The journal keeper will want to record promises made during transactions which later will serve as reminders. They may record impressions of people and situations. The third part of the ministry journal is a summary or reflection about the day. The best ministry journals reflect theological, psychological or sociological principles. Supervisors should write appropriate reactions and return ministry journals in a timely manner.

Not only reports of the task accomplished but also reports of feelings experienced may be important. Mission personnel could write a report of their feelings concerning certain incidents, situations or people, to provide insight to the supervisor and the writer. The conversations in a supervisory conference are confidential unless both decide otherwise. This preserves the integrity of the relationship and makes openness possible.

The supervisory conference ends with the supervisor reviewing the conference discussions and decisions. The supervisor should provide some signal indicating whether the conference went well or not.

3. The post-supervisory conference work. People often ask how much of their time they should plan for a supervisory conference. Usually they mean the encounter during the conference itself. You need to plan for the pre- and post- elements of the conference. The post-supervisory conference work needs to be done immediately after the conference meeting. If not, you will forget details and some of your hunches and feelings about the dynamics.

The supervisor must be alert to responding to language, actions and issues of mission personnel. The supervisor should not be so heavily invested in the agenda that signals given by mission personnel are overlooked. Signals may be in the form of body language (tone of voice, gaze of the eyes or body movement), resistance or compliance.

The best strategy for a supervisor is to debrief about what happened in the conference. The supervisor will mark the calendar for the next conference and other commitments made during the conference. A written account of the supervisory conference should include three categories: facts, feelings and the future.

Facts. The supervisor should record the facts of the supervisory conference. Did the person come prepared? Was he or she late?

Feelings. You will have feelings during and after the conference. These may become important in future conferences or help in determining the patterns. You not only will have feelings but you have a right to them. The point of caution is to keep your feelings separate from the facts. Sometimes you will have hunches that you need to check out in future conferences.

Future. What action do you need to take? What items should you put on the agenda for the next conference? How do you need to intervene in non-productive patterns? How can you affirm the supervisee?

The supervisor's most productive work will revolve around the supervisory conference. Failure to take it seriously will likely blemish otherwise good work.

CHAPTER 7

SUPERVISORY RELATIONSHIPS
AND TEAM BUILDING

One mission supervisor said, "I wish I would never see John Doe again. I tolerate him because it comes with the job. Sometimes I'm not sure it's worth it."

John Doe and the supervisor are fine Christians and effective ministers, but they cannot get along. The supervisor attributes his stomach trouble to his relationship with John Doe. Several times he has tried to get the mission board to dismiss or relocate Doe. Whenever one of them enters a room occupied by the other, you can feel the electricity. This breakdown in their personal relationship has damaged their work effectiveness. They continue to struggle with this mysterious thing called "personal relationship."

Perhaps everyone has secretly wished that a particular deacon would leave the congregation, that a pastor would leave the area, that a staff person would resign or that a student would drop out of school. Even relationships that start off well can sour. How else can we explain the current high divorce rate? People who loved one another and had good, intimate relationships have ended in divorce court. While it may be a positive sign when two people start with a good relationship, they have to work to maintain it.

Relationships are subjective. Insight into oneself and other persons in the relationship is crucial. Supervisors often make the mistake of examining tasks without examining the developing relationship, and the relationship may be a key to team development. Since the greatest supervision tool is the personhood of the supervisor, it is important for the supervisor to feel O.K. about himself or herself. Unhealthy supervisors are likely to create unhealthy people around them.

A GOOD SUPERVISOR
HAS SELF-KNOWLEDGE

Supervisors in touch with themselves are more likely to be effective. Supervisors are not impersonal, neutral computers but persons who bring their personhood to bear upon the supervision role. The supervisor will not understand what is going on in a supervision relationship without self-understanding.

Personal Identity

Supervisors have their own personal identity: who they are; who they are trying to become and who they are in relationship with others. All of us are engaged in moving from adolescence to the various stages of adulthood. We are not at the same place every day or when we face different tasks or persons. When we understand and accept our identity, we will be in a better position to relate to mission personnel.

Supervisors have their own pilgrimages in life and faith. They have particular heritages and views of the future. Each is part of several communities, including home, parental heritage, church and the surrounding secular community. Relationships with those communities determine some of the supervisor's relationships with mission personnel. Supervisors have expectations, feelings and ego needs. Whether or not the supervisors see themselves as having successfully fulfilled these needs will influence the relationships with others. Supervisors have value systems and, while these may differ from supervisor to supervisor, they may easily differ from those of the mission personnel with whom they work.

A supervisor, having grown up during the depression, had a strong Protestant work ethic. His typical week consisted of seven days with twelve hours of work most days. He became the supervisor of a young man who was part of the post-war baby boom and had grown up free of responsibility in a middle-class family. The supervisor and this mission worker clashed over values of work and leisure.

Role Identity

The supervisor's identity relates to a ministry role. A supervisor, who grew up on a farm, never wanted to be anything but a preacher. He carried that goal through college and seminary and reinforced that goal through twenty years of ministry. He preached, visited the sick and bereaved and evangelized the lost. He always wore a business suit and carried a Bible. He became the supervisor of a young man assigned to operate a neighborhood Christian center. The young man had attended college during the days of the hippies and believed in helping people by being a "genuine" person without taking on any role. The supervisor could not understand why the young man did not preach and why he dressed in blue jeans and sandals.

Supervisor's sexual identities also affect the supervision role. In our society there has been a close relationship in the stereotypes of minister's roles and sex roles, but they are now in transition. The male supervisor, who believes a minister's role is determined by sexual identity, may face difficulties when relating to a woman who is ministering. This may be more intense with some persons than with others. One supervisor said, "Don't send me a woman. If I had my way, I wouldn't even have a woman as secretary."

Mission personnel are not the chattel property of the supervisor. Neither is supervision a license to practice psychotherapy.

Supervisors as Ministers
to and with Mission Personnel

The supervisor is a minister both to and with the mission personnel. However else supervisors understand themselves, ministry is the primary role. Mission supervisors have chosen to work with mission personnel and, whatever other roles they have, they are ministers to mission personnel. Of course there is the occasional situation where the mission personnel is sick and requires so much ministry that the supervisor has to forego ministry to other people. When this happens, the supervisor may have to make a tough choice about the on-going relationship with the sick person.

The supervisor also ministers with the mission personnel. A good supervisor is a team builder.

GOOD SUPERVISORS
KNOW THEIR MISSION PERSONNEL

We don't understand ourselves, much less other people. However, there are helps for supervisors who want to understand mission personnel. Each person has a history, an environment and circumstances that are formative. Abilities and their development differ with each person. The successful supervisor examines these areas.

Mission personnel have work and life goals that give clues to their work and behavior. Their ideas will either facilitate or obstruct the supervision process. While supervisors may have similar ideas, they may not have the same intense emotional attachment to those ideas. It facilitates supervision when the supervisor understands the mission personnel's level of commitment to goals and ideas.

Mission personnel relationships with family, other ministers and those in the community will influence their work and relationships. They have self-perceptions that may be realistic, grandiose or self-deprecating. A messianic self-concept will create a different dynamic in the supervision relationship than self-deprecation.

Ways to Examine Supervision Relations

1. Level of intimacy. Growth in the supervisor/mission personnel relationship is important. While they may begin with pleasantries, if they are to work together effectively, they will have to relate on a more substantial basis. Some people can relate on a non-intimate basis quite effectively, but they may be unable to develop intimate relationships.

When people feel O.K. about themselves and others, they are capable of intimate relationships. If they don't, it is impossible to develop intimate relationships. When people feel O.K. about themselves but not O.K. about others, they will run over others. When people do not feel O.K. about themselves but feel others are O.K., they will withdraw, also hindering relationships. The supervision must go beyond the mechanics toward a developing relationship.

2. Supervision of different types of people. People are different from one another. But classification may be so broad or narrow that it distorts rather than depicts reality. Categories, however, can help us understand people and our relationships to them. For instance, J. W. Thomas, a business consultant and psychologist, developed Bi/Polar psychology. He noticed in working with businesses that the people were either thinkers or doers. The thinkers were either factual or theoretical. The doers were relational or independent. He recognized that all have equal value, and all are equally needed by our society. While a person operates out of a particular stance, most have abilities in all of the areas. People may be dependent, factual thinkers; independent, factual thinkers; dependent, theoretical thinkers; independent, theoretical thinkers; factual, relational persons; theoretical, relational persons; factual, independent or theoretical, independent persons.

Two members of a congregation's staff were talented, well-trained Christian men but were in constant conflict. While they had separate responsibilities, many tasks brought them into direct conflict. Upon analysis, the minister of education and youth found that he was an independent, aloof and theoretical person. He always formulated creative ideas for dealing with problems. The minister of music was a warm, relational, factual person. The minister of education and youth saw the way things could be; the minister of music dealt with things the way they were. By understanding their differences, hostility began to subside and a new partnership developed. One did not acquiesce to the other. Instead, they understood the source of the problem and were able to take their individual strengths into account. They also found they could use not only their natural strengths but also their secondary strengths.

The ideal, therefore, is not for two people to be alike, but for them to work within creative tension. The supervisor needs to look at the relationship with mission personnel to determine their differences. It is not always healthy for two people who are different to divide tasks according to strengths. People need to exercise the relative strengths they have in other areas.

3. Patterns of relationships in supervision. Many patterns develop in the supervisor/mission personnel relationships. Taken individually, any of these patterns is understandable. In certain situations, they may be appropriate. The supervisor needs to initiate examination of patterns in relationships developed in the supervisory situation. If the supervisor finds one pattern has become normative, he or she should ask the question "why" in order to determine the appropriateness of a developed pattern. Patterns may meet the needs of either the supervisor or the mission personnel or both, rather than just the needs of supervision. They include:

Confrontation: an open disagreement. The supervisor needs to determine whether there is always a confrontation or avoidance of confrontation on the part of the supervisor or mission personnel.

Dependency. One person constantly leans upon another rather than developing his/her own autonomy.

Intimidation. One person overwhelms another by either overt or tacit threats. This may be the attempt of official authority to elicit power.

Rejection. One person may rule out the other. Confrontation does not occur and issues are not worked out.

Projection. One person imputes to the other ideas and feelings which do not belong to the other person.

Transference. One attributes feelings to another as if the other person is responsible for those feelings.

Countertransference. One person assumes and deals with the feelings thought to be feelings which the other person is dealing with.

Supervisors need to monitor their own ways of dealing with these patterns. Are they acting passively, aggressively, passive-aggressively or assertively? The passive person may acquiesce, allowing things to happen. The aggressive person may act without consideration for the rights and feelings of others. The passive-aggressive person may at first acquiesce and later find a way to "get even." The assertive person initiates strongly, yet acknowledges and considers the feelings and rights of others.

The supervisor may also monitor the relationship as to patterns corresponding to common experience. Is the relationship that of a father and son, of friends or partners, etc.? Is relationship to mission personnel that of errand boy, alter-ego, student or child?

GAMES THAT AFFECT RELATIONSHIPS

People need to deal straightforwardly with their personalities and agendas in relationships. Playing games interferes with directness and openness. If games are played, it is difficult to know the other person and the existing relationship.

Supervision is not just looking over the facts and figures presented to the supervisor. It is two people engaged in a meaningful relationship. The supervisor is responsible for monitoring that relationship. Both the supervisor and mission personnel are responsible for facilitating the most productive relationship.

"A church like ours can't put on a stewardship program. All of those stewardship programs sent out by the denomination are for large churches, not a little mission church like ours," said Reverend John Doe to his supervisor. The supervisor insisted denominational programs exist for small congregations and requested that the state stewardship director contact Rev. Doe. Doe continued to object but half-heartedly put on the program. The program was not very successful. Afterwards John Doe met with his supervisor and said, "The people are discouraged because the stewardship program did not turn out too well. I wish I had never heard of that stupid program. I wish you had never sent that stewardship director."

Rev. Doe was game-playing. Unfortunately, games do not help anyone. The supervisor was concerned, the congregation did not have a successful program, Rev. Doe had not learned how to conduct a stewardship program, nor did the church have any stronger financial base.

Games are ulterior transactions with payoffs. The payoff in this game was that Rev. Doe shifted his responsibility to another person, his supervisor. Games may be used to avoid or shift responsibility, to gain reassurance or to manipulate others' attitudes or actions. Games are played constantly. No one is exempt. No one is a real winner. Most games get in the way of relationships, communication and work.

Games Supervisees Play

While game-playing is common to both supervisee and supervisor, below are games more common to the supervisee.

1. Supervisory split. The supervisory split is possible where shared supervision involves more than one agency and/or supervisor. National, state and local agencies, cooperating in a mission project, are vulnerable to this game. When one mission appointee was urged by the national Home Mission Board to attend a conference but his local supervisor was not in favor of it, he reminded the local supervisor that the Home Mission Board paid a great deal of his salary and insisted on his attendance. When he did not want to attend such a conference, he told the Home Mission Board that his local supervisor would not allow him to attend. This man knew how to use the supervisory split.

The supervisory split clouds the process of supervision. Multiple supervisors need to communicate with one another in order to keep clear lines of accountability. This is one reason why supervisors should provide supervisor reports to those who supervise them.

2. Let's you and him fight. Mission personnel use the game "Let's you and him fight" by pitting the supervisor against someone else. This may even lead to a supervisory split. The mission personnel may resist his/her supervisor by appealing to another supervisor, an expert or a person in his/her field of ministry. Mission personnel may pit the supervisor against tradition, doctrine, creed or confession of faith.

3. Wooden leg. "What do you expect from a man with a wooden leg?" A person playing "wooden leg" points to some problem, personal or institutional, in order to avoid responsibility. Mission personnel may use circumstances, financial resources or the few lay supervisors in the mission as their "wooden leg."

A supervisor facing the "wooden leg" game needs to help mission personnel get in touch with reality. He needs to help them on their gifts rather than their limitations. Secondly, mission personnel should realize doing the job means overcoming obstacles and limitations.

4. Look how hard I've tried. Since the Protestant work ethic rewards hard work, dealing with this game is especially difficult. Mission personnel may prove the number of meetings held, the visits made or the paperwork handled. And while hard work is admirable, the question remains, "Did it produce the desired outcomes?" The covenant between supervisor and mission personnel should spell out goals. Mission personnel are responsible not only for activities, but for reaching goals. Sometimes it is easier to work than to achieve. This is especially true if the work shown by mission personnel is paperwork.

5. Clown. The "clown" uses humor to keep people at an arm's distance. After all, who can seriously attack someone in a good humor who evokes laughter? The supervisor must let the supervisee know that he or she is accountable for goals met, not for charm and wit.

6. Kick me. This game is played by the person's admission to a fault or to the fact that people always blame him or her. The nature of the blunder may be exaggerated; then comes the invitation, "kick me." This puts the supervisor between a rock and a hard place. Usually, the player makes a tempting "offer" and the supervisor may feel inclined to oblige. But if the agenda has been suggested by the other person, the supervisor is no longer in charge. And who wants to take the advice ("kick me") of someone who has not shown the best judgment in the past? The other side of the dilemma is if the supervisor lets the person off the hook, he or she fails to control the agenda.

One supervisee who played "kick me" had a difficult childhood. He reviewed all the problems he had experienced when he failed to meet performance standards and implied, "Everybody else has kicked me; now it is your turn." On the day that we were to meet, I faced a dilemma. Mere confrontation concerning his failures to perform was insufficient supervision. He had to be confronted on the basis of his game-playing. Although he was bright, talented and energetic, he was playing both "kick me" and "wooden leg." He began to realize he would be held accountable for his ability rather than his problems.

7. Stupid. The person who plays "stupid" tries to get you to commiserate with him at his clumsiness and ineptitude. This person wants forgiveness by naming the clumsiness before the supervisor does. This takes away the supervisor's ammunition. Who can kick somebody who is already down?

8. Why does this always happen to me? This game indicates the player has no control over life and is in the hands of fate. This person brags of misfortune and accepts the loser's syndrome. Like Naomi in the Old Testament, who asked people to call her Mara (which means "bitter"), this person majors in tragedy.

Mission personnel playing this game need empathetic and life-changing support. If mission personnel understand psychology, the supervisor may point out that this life script asks for difficulties; only from disappointments and even tragedies does the person derive satisfaction. This person needs to be encouraged not to give up in the face of real difficulties and to meet imagined needs for sympathy in other ways. The supervisee should examine alternative reasons for tragic events. (The person is accident prone; disappointments are common to all persons, this person is responsible, etc.) In the event of real game playing, the supervisor needs to hold the person accountable.

9. Harried. Perhaps other than the harried housewife, there is no one who typifies this characterization more than the minister. Ministry demands a wide range of expertise. The work load is heavy. The goal of reaching the world (or even the community) for Christ is awesome. And perhaps mission personnel are the most harried of all. Often they do menial chores connected with their usual ministerial chores. The harried mission personnel jumps from one job to another, unable to complete a task and failing to achieve results or meet goals. To this person, being busy may mean being important. Or the person may operate out of an "adaptive child" ego state which tries to please everyone.

The supervisor needs to emphasize this person's self-worth so service involves a "worthy" sacrifice. This person could keep a ministry journal for evaluation of time use to discover meaning in action. This could cut down on the number of tasks in which the person becomes compulsively involved.

10. Psychiatry. This game can be broken down into two kinds of games. In the first, the person infers, "I am a minister and a healer. If you do not get well, it is your fault." Or, "I am a minister called of God and educated to be the leader; therefore, this is what you ought to do."

The people to whom the mission personnel relate sometimes play a game of acquiescence, responding, "You are the healer and, therefore, I will be well," whether or not that healing takes place. A person called of God is under constraint to offer assertive supervision. However, it becomes a game when the person depends upon credentials alone. In the second phase of "psychiatry," a person tries to solve the problem by labeling behavior. Calling someone neurotic may identify a problem, but it is not ministry.

11. Uproar. This game creates diversion and avoidance. It is an avenue for escaping accountability. During a conference about one man's failure to fulfill his covenant, the man in question turned to the supervisor and accused him of not keeping confidence. Whenever pressed for a way to resolve his problems, the man said he could not trust the confidentiality of his supervisor. Mission personnel may use issues such as doctrine, policy, lack of concern or failure of agencies to cause "uproar."

Years ago when the number of baptisms declined in a particular state, the state evangelism secretary campaigned all over the state against the "heresy" he found in a seminary professor's book. He created enough "uproar" that people forgot about the declining baptismal rate.

The supervisor should concentrate on one problem at a time and get the facts. The supervisor may suggest handling the "uproar" issue only after dealing with the issue at hand. Supervisors dealing with the uproar first have lost control of their supervisory role.

12. Spiritualizing. This game is a great deal like "psychiatry." The difference is that "spiritualizing" uses God-talk. The point is "How can you attack anyone so holy?" Mission personnel, revered highly for their sacrificial service, are particularly susceptible to this game. They may use such phrases as "God's will," "the Lord led," and "God blessed." These concepts are legitimate signs of game playing if they hinder solving the problem by labeling behavior. Calling someone neurotic may identify a problem, but it is not ministry.

Supervisors generally respond in two ways: the abrasive approach is to say something like: "O.K., I've heard all of your gobbledegook; now tell me what happened in everyday English;" or the supervisor can affirm a personal belief in spirituality and then ask for the account in human terms which would communicate to an outsider.

13. Blemish. The game "blemish" finds flaws in the other person, and disqualifies the person from significant supervisory relationship. The person will spar like a boxer in the opening round, find the blemish, then exploit that flaw whenever the supervisor raises significant agenda. While it may never be verbalized, the implication is "If you are so smart, why aren't you . . ." "If you are that good, you ought to be president of the Southern Baptist Convention." Or "How many souls did you win last year?"

This intimidating game can only be dealt with head on. The supervisor should point out the realities of the situation—that he or she has been appointed supervisor because of their position, perhaps, rather than expertise and this is a responsibility he/she intends to fulfill. The supervisor may confront the mission personnel, saying, "Are you saying that you do not think that I can help you with this issue?" If the mission personnel denies the insinuation, the supervisor should take the initiative, asking, "How can I help then?" If the mission personnel does not believe the supervisor can help, the supervisor needs to ask, "Who might be able to help?" Ultimately, mission personnel must view themselves as accountable.

14. If it weren't for you. Mission personnel may try to shift the responsibility for their problems to the supervisor (as in the example at the beginning of this chapter about the less-than-successful stewardship program). Mission personnel with fragile egos may not be able to handle failure. Supervision should occur within the context of support in which mission personnel feel secure.

The supervisor may assume part of the responsibility and then ask the mission personnel, "What was your responsibility in this failure and from this point on how are _you_ going to assume responsibility for this situation?" The issue is not to find who is to blame but to help the person take the initiative to make things happen and assume the responsibility for what happens.

15. If I only had. This game attributes problems to external conditions. "If I only had enough money," "if we only had a good building," "if the mission board would just let us do so and so," or "if it weren't so far away" are frequently made statements common to this game.

The potential for game playing makes covenant goals very important. No one should hold mission personnel accountable for accomplishment beyond their resources. The covenant between supervisor and mission personnel should spell out goals within the realm of available resources.

16. Corner. "Corner" involves a double bind. Mission personnel put the supervisor in a corner. When the supervisor asks why a task is not complete, they might respond, "You told me to spend more time with the family and not to work so hard."

17. Ain't it awful. In this game, mission personnel (or supervisor) discuss the "terrible state" of people or conditions. They attempt to elicit a sympathetic acquiescence from the supervisor with: "Ain't it awful about young people today," "ain't it awful what the communists are doing," or "ain't it awful about the liberals (or fundamentalists)." This conversation precludes supervisory issues. Also, if supervisors disagree, the tacit threat looms they may become the object of "ain't it awful."

Because he or she likes adulation, the supervisor may overlook the fact that nothing has been done about the subject. In fact, under these conditions it is difficult for the supervisor to confront mission personnel. After all, how ungrateful can a supervisor be?

Games Supervisors Play

The supervisors, while capable of playing any of the games which mission personnel play, seem more vulnerable to particular games because of the supervision. They may play "blemish," seeking a flaw in the mission personnel in order to discount the person's worth. "Look how hard I've tried" is tempting when supervision goes sour. The supervisor not meeting role responsibilities may play the game "harried," complaining about the number of tasks.

"Psychiatry" is also a favorite game because it is easier to label a person than to guide him or her to productivity. The supervisor with low ego strength may play "stupid" to avoid responsibility. The supervisor may play "I'm only trying to help you." Rather than adequately supervising, the supervisor appeals to mission personnel's sympathy or guilt.

The issue of games is important in supervision and communication. Games can get in the way of both. The supervisor should take time outside the supervisory setting to examine interplay with the mission personnel. Supervisors should also ask their supervisors if they detect any games between mission personnel and themselves.

Many of these games are not limited to the supervisory relationship but continue through life. Eric Berne described many of the games in his book, *Games People Play*. The psychological background of the games is presented in Berne's book.

TEAM BUILDING

Team building is a major function of a supervisor whether she or he supervises one or many. A team can accomplish more than a number of individuals working by themselves. Team building is a delicate exercise; a team can shatter into individuals easily.

The Team and Relationships

Members of the team must respect one another or the team will be dysfunctional. Good relationships help the team work. This does not mean just good feelings but appreciation of the roles and gifts of each team member.

Teams as Support Groups

The team is important in getting jobs done, but it also serves as a support group. The team learns to care for and support one another. This brings greater depth to the sense of fulfillment. This is applicable to volunteers as well as paid staff. Since support is an important element in supervision, the team assists in supervision.

States and Team Building

The states of supervision (see chapter 5) provide help in understanding team building. Fully integrated teams appear in the partnership state. In the structure and cooperative states there can be teams, but they are limited to joining the team of the supervisor. The supervisor is the central figure in these states, doing most of the decision making and assigning of tasks. The fellowship state usually provides for a kind of consensus process. The partnership state is the state where the team is mature with mutual give and take between the supervisor and supervisee. Here the supervisee is a team partner rather than just a member of the supervisor's team.

Several situations limit the development of the mature team. One is crises. Where there is a crisis, the team leader may have to exercise more direct team leadership than otherwise necessary. When a supervisee is young, the supervisor will have to limit team building to the structure state. During the early stage of supervision, the alert supervisor will limit the team process to the structure and cooperative states. This will allow the supervisee to learn the system, develop skills and "earn" his or her way onto the team.

Development in Team Building

Teams develop through stages. One writer has suggested four stages of development (however, I have taken some liberties with them). [1] The first stage of team building is to "form." The people of the team get together either by the supervisor recruiting or by a group recognizing the need of a team to address a problem. This stage often carries enthusiasm about the situation or position.

The second stage of team development is "storm." Differences begin to appear after the team forms. The supervisee discovers differences with the supervisor's philosophy or procedures. If a group decides to create a team to deal with a problem, they find that their understandings or approaches are different. When the team members are aggressive or assertive, the storm period can be overt (and even loud). Passive-aggressive people may "guinea-sack" their responses but find a way to sabotage the team.

When the team members spend some time storming, the common values begin to appear and they go to the "norm" stage. They may find that they have enough in common to go ahead with the team. A supervisee may realize that he or she has not arrived in Camelot but still can work as a team member.

The last stage is "perform." The team members are able to work together to accomplish the task or function in the position as team members. This is realism since most people have to compromise in order to be members of a team. There are limits to the compromising. They cannot compromise major principles. The supervisee may find that his or her reason for joining the team is negated by the compromise and will have to withdraw. Supervisors have sometimes realized that they will do better by themselves rather than doing constant battle with a volunteer who cannot find common ground for working as a team member. However, teams do perform after they have come to understand that each member will have to compromise.

---

[1] E. Mansell Pattison, *Pastor and Parish—a Systems Approach* (Philadelphia: Fortress Press, 1977), pp. 58-62, 88.

Dangers in Team Building

The dangers in team building may be especially disconcerting to the impatient and aggressive supervisor who wants to get the "show on the road." Development always takes time. The situation and the people determine how long team development will take. People may also get stuck in a stage and slow the process. Some may celebrate the forming stage rather than get to the hard work. The storming stage may frighten some and impede progress. If this stage is not handled correctly, people may be hurt and slow or even stop the process. Reflective people may enjoy the norming stage and fail to move into the performing stage as they should.

A temptation is to try to skip a stage. Many people avoid conflict when possible so they are reluctant to invest in the storming stage. Impatient people may not want to go through the norming stage but plunge into the performing stage. If the supervisor has been through the norming stage before and has worked out the norming issues, he or she should remember than the supervisee probably has not been through this stage. It is important for both to go through it together. Team loyalty develops with the process as members learn to work together.

When a team adds another team member, the team has to start all over in the developmental process with the new team member. If they do not, the new person never really joins the team. The supervisor who has gone through the process with one team and moves to another team has to start over in the developmental process. The temptation is for supervisors to want to start with the new team at the stage where they were with the previous team. When a team takes on a new task, they also have to start over with the developmental process. Hopefully their previous experience will enable them to develop more rapidly into the new team for the new task.

Gifts Team Members Offer

Team members bring different gifts to the team. Their talents and experiences help the team to do many things one person could not accomplish. Paul lists many gifts in 1 Corinthians 12.

We cannot expect to be equal in our gifts. Some people are better equipped with some gifts than others.

Psychologists have developed inventories to help us determine our gifts and patterns of functioning. Inventories, such as the Myers Briggs Temperament Inventory, help us discern our functioning patterns. The team needs persons with a variety of gifts in order to accomplish goals. A team with all "thinkers" will have difficulty getting tasks done. A team may need administrators, sales people, entrepreneurs and a field marshal. If everyone on the team is only one of these, they may understand each other but fail to do all the team's tasks well. The effective supervisor may seek people with a variety of gifts and patterns to create the team.

SUMMARY

The superior supervisor will not overlook the importance of relationships in the supervisory process. The supervisor will need to give regular attention to the relationships as well as the work. Good relationships not only make working together more pleasant but more productive. Supervisory relationships are not always intimate, but the quality of the relationships must be strong.

CHAPTER 8

CROSS-CULTURAL SUPERVISION

Multiple cultures have changed the nature of supervision. Not only do foreign missionaries face cross-cultural supervision when working with nationals, but many supervisors in American religious institutions deal with cross-cultural supervision because of the many ethnic groups in the United States. Although there is often discomfort in supervising personnel from one's own cultural background, new situations emerge when supervision is cross cultural. Successful supervision depends on understanding so the cultural backgrounds provide part of the scenario for good supervision. This chapter provides clues to several areas in cross-cultural supervision.

SYNCRETISM

A Christian has to worry about the possibility of distorting the gospel through cultural syncretism. Syncretism is the coalescence or uniting of two different religious beliefs. When syncretism happens, Christianity can lose its distinctive character. However, all belief is clothed in some culture (or cultures). The gospel is never naked but is always clothed in some cultural garb. It is important for people to clothe the gospel in their culture, but it is also crucial for that cultural clothing to express the gospel rather than hide the gospel.

Foreign missionaries face this challenge in most cultures where they serve, but it is not exclusively a non-American challenge because there are many ethnics and sub-cultures within the United States. Nowhere is this clearer than in the music used in worship that ranges from Bach to spirituals and from country-western to rock.

Scripture is a check against syncretism. Faithful adherence to scripture principles provide a measure of protection against syncretism. The only deterrent is the improper interpretation of Scripture that may create barriers to reaching across culture or compromise a critical point of Scripture. The Holy Spirit is one of the helps for interpreting Scripture and being sensitive to God and people.

The church also provides help against syncretism since the collective wisdom and communal divine leadership serves as a check against individualism. The church is not only the current Kingdom members but those past saints who have left a rich heritage of faith for Christians to follow. They have often addressed issues in their times that reappear in future generations.

READING CULTURAL DIFFERENCES

The supervisor who works with a person born in the United States and speaks English fluently may believe that they share a common cultural heritage, but the supervisor may be badly mistaken. An urbane New Yorker differs greatly from an Ozark hillbilly. Reading cultural differences is imperative for the good supervisor. Cultural differences are more than language and accent differences. A foreign mission leader has said:

When the person who has never been outside of the USA first arrives (in a foreign country), often his or her expectations of life in another country are very idealistic and naive. This may be especially true if this person has had a college friend or close acquaintance with a national from that country who has had an extended stay in the USA. Little does the foreign visitor realize that the nationals will not be like this person who has become more "Americanized" or "internationalized." So the first shock is that "these people are different from what I expected."

It is easy to misread cultural issues. Supervisors may not

get beyond the politeness of a supervisee to learn the different "psyche" that forms his or her opinions, judgments and actions.

LANGUAGE

Language is the most obvious element in cultural differences. When we hear a different accent or grammatical sentence construction, we immediately have a signal that there is a cultural issue.   Even when people use the right words, we cannot assume that they mean exactly what we mean by them. The good supervisor will examine language carefully.   Every culture has words that are not used in polite company, but they may be innocent words in another culture.

VALUES

All cultural groups do not have the same values. Recently I talked with a foreign missionary about a certain tribe.   He provided the assessment that they placed a low value on human life.   The Euro-American society is very materialistic.   Other cultures have difficulty understanding the American emphasis upon budgets and audits. The family is a supreme value among some cultures. They place the family above individual rights.

Americans think of anyone having citizenship in the United States as an American.   However, Greeks tend to see Greeks anywhere as a part of the Greek culture and religion. Chinese see Chinese descendants anywhere in the world as Chinese. Their value systems are more "racial" than national.

The Texan may be impressed by how big something is, while the New Englander is more impressed by how old it is. A man from the hill country of Eastern Kentucky once threatened to bring his shotgun to church and shoot all the people leading his wife astray. A neighbor, commenting on the threat, said, "At least he's a good worker."   The community largely judged people on the basis of their industriousness.

A professor used to tell the story of four scholars from Germany, France, Britain, and the United States who agreed to write essays on elephants. The German produced five huge volumes entitled, "A Short Introduction to the History of

Elephants." The French scholar had a small booklet, tied in a pink ribbon, entitled, "The Love Life of Elephants." The British scholar produced a volume entitled, "Elephants in the Empire." The American wrote a book entitled, "How to Grow Bigger and Better Elephants." Cultural values affect how we approach subjects.

FAMILY

Family values is the politically correct thing to talk about today. Many Christian religious groups are leading the family values discussions. However, there are cultures where family is much more central to life and thought than in the United States. It is not a question of family values but the family itself that is central and sacred. Some Asian cultures worship their ancestors. Accepting Christianity not only means changing religion but turning one's back on the family — not only the present family but one's whole family heritage. While that is true, people from these cultures still have emotional ties, if not spiritual ties, with their family and ancestry. When a supervisor communicates with the supervisee from a family centered culture, the communication is with the whole family, not just with the supervisee.

WORK

The Protestant work ethic, brought to America by the Puritans, is part of the American heritage. In its pure form, work is an absolute value rather than a utilitarian necessity. Cultures that have not been influenced by the Puritan tradition will probably have a different view of work. These cultures may see work only as utilitarian. They may have values that place manual labor only in the hands of lower classes.

Some Chinese students attending a seminary in the United States could not understand the willingness of American students to work in factories near the seminary doing assembly line work. The Chinese students were willing to work in the seminary library because that was culturally acceptable for "scholars," but assembly line work was not acceptable. The supervisor, even if not a workaholic, may not understand the different attitude toward work by a person from another culture.

AUTHORITY

American democratization has changed attitudes toward authority. Individualism has replaced absolute authority of officials. Some cultures have a history of autocratic governments as well as autocratic family relationships. Usually this autocracy is reflected in religious life which makes it difficult for the people to feel comfortable with a congregational polity. In some cultures the authority factor is age so that the oldest man is the authority of the community. When translated into the religious community, the oldest minister is the leader of the religious community.

The person who gets supervisory authority from position may not understand why there are supervisory problems with a person from an autocratic culture. A supervisor who is younger than an Asian supervisee may experience resistance from the supervisee.

Authority is more complex where women are concerned. There are many cultures where the woman is under the near absolute authority of her father until her marriage and, after marriage, to her husband. The supervisor may face resistance from the woman supervisee because she understands that her husband is the final authority for what she does. She may not be free to attend meetings or set priorities the same as her supervisor. Because of the politeness in her cultural background, she may not be able to confront the supervisor.

So the supervisor is counting on her to fulfill what he understands to be commitments on her part, but she has only been polite in saying "yes" when she may not be free to follow up. The supervisor can seriously damage the marital relationship or the professional status of the supervisee unless he or she understands the cultural situation and finds a way to handle it.

TIME

The Euro-American world places great emphasis on time, but

that sentiment is not universal. Europe has trains that run on a schedule that seldom varies by a minute. Television operates on the basis of seconds. Computers are often measured in nanoseconds. An atomic clock keeps time so accurately that it will not lose a second in centuries. This obsession with time is not shared by many cultures.

Some cultures see time as important only as related to events. Sequential time is not as important as consequential time. This is more like the notion of time among the early Hebrews who were likely to measure time by events such as in Isaiah 6, where the event was recalled as being "in the year that King Uzziah died."

The supervisor who operates on the Western concept of time can experience conflict when working with supervisees from other cultures. Deadlines may pass and reports may not be forthcoming. The supervisor may interpret these behaviors as resistance or lack of interest or poor discipline. Rather than becoming trapped by these misinterpretations, the good supervisor will map a strategy for working with the person who has a different concept of time.

COMMUNICATION

Communication involves language but goes beyond it. Some cultures trust only communication that is direct while others depend on circuitous locution. Body language is different among cultures. Gestures mean different things in various cultures. A thumb-up sign in America means a good job or O.K. but in Japan and Germany they use thumbs in counting. Knocking on a door of a house is a way Americans call the attention of the house's residents, but in some cultures you stand outside and clap your hands.

Not all cultures shake hands. Some press their palms together in a praying stance. Shaking hands is different among cultures. A Texan may think a soft handshake is a sign of a wimp, but some Asian groups prefer a gentle handshake because a firm shake denotes aggressiveness.

Loud conversation with extravagant gesturing is typical of some cultures, while others are offended by such behavior, appreciating only controlled behavior. If you don't look an Ozarker in the eyes, he doesn't believe you, but it is an insult to look directly into the eyes of a Native American when talking. On the other hand, not to look an elderly Chinese in the eye is a faux pas.   Some cultures communicate normally through conversation and shun letters and memos.

Communication is crucial to supervision so the effective supervisor will check the communication process carefully when working with a person from another culture.   Memos may be ignored while oral communication will bring rewards.

CLOTHING

A young missionary fresh from college arrived on a foreign mission field. He was outgoing with a ready laugh. His normal dress was jeans, T-shirt and a blue knit toboggan cap that he wore at all times whether at meals or in his quarters. His long hair appeared from under his blue cap. His assignment was to teach English, and his first class was a group of government employees and civil servants who had been sent by the province chief. When the young missionary was introduced wearing his jeans, T-shirt and blue cap, a nervous twitter went through the class.

Each culture has its view of appropriate dress. Apparel that is not appreciated by the supervisor may be the normal clothing among the groups with whom the supervisee works. It may be necessary for the supervisor and supervisee to determine what clothing is appropriate in different circumstances. The person working in a soup kitchen may need to be sensitive about dress when appearing before a group of business persons who are funding the work.

LOGIC

Socratic thinking and Aristotelian logic are not universal. Groups may make decisions on the basis of people or tradition. People base decisions on deductions or inferences from previous experience. Where a world-view is different, logical inferences will be different.   While the Euro-American world is accustomed to "scientific" thinking, other groups are not; they look for causes that are not explained by linear thinking or primary causes.

RELIGION

Each culture has a religion that has its own rites, ceremonies, holy objects and persons. Some of these religions have been part of the culture for thousands of years. The culture and religion are so intertwined that they cannot exist without each other. Whatever the religion, it deals with some basic issues such as origins, relationships, death and destiny. Rituals and ceremonies reflect how the culture has related to these in their history. People have been shaped by the rituals and ceremonies in their culture. Understanding people from another culture means understanding how their religious heritage has shaped them.

SUMMARY

Supervisors often suffer from not having studied anthropology during their academic programs. Whether that is a possibility or not, a good supervisor of persons from another culture (or sub-culture) will find a way to understand cultural issues and incorporate this sensitivity into his or her cross-cultural supervision.

CHAPTER 9

SUPERVISING VOLUNTEERS

Democratic societies depend on volunteers. Most capable Americans do volunteer work in churches, civic organizations, professional societies or youth groups. Few institutions could afford to staff their organizations fully with paid personnel. No one can estimate the importance and contributions volunteers have made to American institutions. Pastors may forget that churches are staffed largely by volunteers serving as Sunday School teachers, deacons and committee members.

Fortunately, most volunteers make a positive contribution. Occasionally a volunteer creates problems. When I spoke to a foreign missionary about volunteers serving on foreign mission fields, she reacted strongly about problems her mission had experienced. She told me that the stress of a new culture caused one volunteer to "crack up" and even attack a local authority. She said that missionaries had to take turns "baby sitting" him until they could get him out of the country. This was a case of a volunteer not only interfering with mission work but actually threatening the status of missionaries living in that country.

This chapter will provide structure for using volunteers that will help supervisors make the experiences of volunteers positive and affirming. Supervisors sometimes want a volunteer to do a job without spending time and energy with the volunteer. That is unrealistic. A good supervisor will invest in the preparation, training and directing of the volunteer. The supervisor who doesn't give attention to the volunteer situation courts disappointment or maybe even disaster.

There will be resistance to structure for volunteers by those who claim that you can't require anything from volunteers because you don't pay them. However, volunteerism requires a different perspective. You have no business with a person or volunteer whom you can't incorporate into the discipline of your system. You can compensate volunteers even when money is not the issue.

Ministers usually claim that they don't do their work for the money but for the satisfaction which comes from serving God and God's people. Volunteers look for satisfaction beyond money; it is this satisfaction which the supervisor can provide. The ministry setting does reward the volunteer by providing a sense of worth. This gives the supervisor leverage for structuring the relationship with the volunteer.

PREPARING FOR VOLUNTEERS

A good volunteer situation doesn't "just happen." It takes preparation on the part of the supervisor. The preparation is partly personal and partly institutional.

Spiritual

The supervisor who has a servant attitude is spiritually prepared for a volunteer. This supervisor will minister to the volunteer instead of using the volunteer for personal gratification.

Psychological

When relating to volunteers, the supervisor's state of mind is important. Business will not be as usual. The volunteer will need some of the supervisor's time. There will be a new person with whom to share information, responsibility, authority and appreciation.

System

Before the new volunteer begins, the smart supervisor will

inform other volunteers and staff about the new person and his or her role. People already in the system will feel better with the appropriate information and will be less threatened if the supervisor informs them about the new volunteer ahead of time.

Goals

When supervisors or institutions develop goals, they enhance the selection and success of volunteers. There are times when people want a volunteer because of prestige or believing that another person will solve the institutional problems. An institution without goals probably doesn't need a volunteer.

Job Description

A volunteer deserves a job description as much as a paid staff member. It not only adds dignity to the volunteer's work, but it also provides help in directing the volunteer and making sure the volunteer doesn't interfere with the work of others. The job description will help the volunteer to know whether he or she has the gifts and interest to become involved. If a job is worth doing, it deserves a job description.

Recruit

Lovers want to be pursued. You need to recruit volunteers. It makes them feel wanted. Recruiting is more than putting a note in a bulletin requesting help. Recruiting gives the supervisor the opportunity to define the situation rather than accept the terms of the volunteer. When you recruit, you have the opportunity to motivate the volunteers at the beginning by letting them know they are wanted.

Train

An axiom of supervision is, "If you refuse to train, you won't serve." Training is necessary to provide skills, orient to a job and to make a person a part of the team. There are several levels of training. One level is to train the person for the tasks he or she will do. This may be extensive, or it could take only one session. A second level of training is to help a volunteer take his or her skills and adapt them to the work situation. A third training level is orientation to the institution and its policies. A nurse, for example, has professional training but needs to know about the routine and policies of the well-baby clinic where he or she will volunteer to help low-income families.

It is important to insist on training for the sake of others on the team. They will feel betrayed by you if you allow a volunteer to work without paying the price of training.

Covenant

The covenant is as important to the volunteer as any paid staff. The covenant is not a job description that deals with only the tasks. The covenant relates to the personal needs and goals as well as the tasks. The covenant will be central in the evaluation. The mature volunteer will be able to initiate more of the covenant than an inexperienced person.

WORKING WITH VOLUNTEERS

Assign

The supervisor assigns the volunteer to responsibilities. Clear communication is important between the supervisor and volunteer and also between the supervisor and others in the system. Everyone needs to know the role, authority and responsibilities of the volunteer. The volunteer needs a title to carry out the assignment.

Delegate

Delegation can be difficult. Many supervisors have trouble "letting go" and making delegation real. Supervisors feel the need to hold on even when they have competent volunteers. Real delegation means assigning tasks and giving the necessary authority for fulfilling the responsibilities to a supervisee.

Initiate

The moment of truth comes for the volunteer when he or she has to begin the assignment. Tasks that are second nature to the supervisor may be new for the volunteer. The helpful supervisor goes with the volunteer for the first task (or perhaps several) to make the volunteer feel comfortable and at home with the process and the tasks.

Provide

Many volunteers have complained about not having the resources needed to fulfill their assignments. This is true in Sunday School and Vacation Bible School as well as other forms of volunteer ministry. The supervisor will be especially helpful if he or she checks regularly with the volunteer about resources.

Supervise

The supervisor's responsibility remains throughout the assignment. It begins with the covenant, carries through regular supervisory conferences and concludes with the evaluation. This is a period when the supervisor should monitor the volunteer's work and continue to motivate the volunteer.

Evaluate

The conclusion of the volunteer's work is an evaluation. The covenant will be the guide for directing the review of the volunteer's experience. If it is appropriate, the supervisor and volunteer may wish to continue the relationship and will create a new covenant for this new phase.

SPECIAL SITUATIONS
WITH SHORT-TERM VOLUNTEERS

Short-term volunteers present special situations for supervisors. These show up especially with regard to the covenant and supervisory conferences.

Short-term Covenants

When people are going to be working on a short-term basis, the covenant will be more task-oriented. The supervisor will not be able to get acquainted with a work crew well enough in a week's time to deal with personhood issues.

If a crew is going to work on a building or a youth group plans to present a musical one night or teach in a vacation Bible school for a week, the supervisor relates to the leader of the group rather than all the persons in the group. The whole group is the leader's responsibility. The supervisor relates to the leader.

A prudent supervisor will make a covenant with the leader of a work team or a youth group. The leader of the group should go to the place where the group will minister several months before the group arrives in order to see the setting and the facilities and to make a covenant with the supervisor. Sometimes there is resistance to the expenditure of time and money the visit will cost. However, a team that can afford to travel can afford for the leader to meet with the supervisor at the scene of ministry. If the team resists this investment, you can fear their future investment in the ministry at your site.

Supervisory Conferences
with Short-Term Volunteers

The supervisory conference will follow the pattern of the short-term covenant and be task-oriented. The covenant dealt with task issues so the conference should deal with task issues.

The supervisory conference will be between the supervisor and the leader of the volunteer group. The supervisor is vulnerable to meddling if he or she tries to supervise any members of the team. The leader is responsible to the supervisor, and the team is responsible to the leader.

Task-oriented but Sensitive

While the supervisor deals with the task issues and only with the leader, the supervisor should be sensitive to team members as persons. There will be times when a team member faces a spiritual or personal problem. Being away from home gives the volunteer psychic space to reflect on his or her situation, and thus he or she may have the need for counsel or guidance. The volunteer may even need someone to listen who is not involved with him or her "back home." The supervisor's sensitivity may lead to a significant ministry with a short-term volunteer.

CONCLUSION

Volunteers are special persons and precious resources. We should treat them with respect. They deserve all the attention and ministry we give to other co-workers.

CHAPTER 10

SPECIAL
SUPERVISORY SITUATIONS

When asked to name supervisory problems, participants in supervision workshops respond with enough answers to fill a chalkboard. This chapter deals with specific problems encountered by supervisors and mission personnel. Problem-free supervision is probably not even desirable. As supervisor and mission personnel work out their supervisory problems, they model and practice the art of problem-solving which the mission personnel can use in their ministry setting. If supervision appears to be problem-free, either supervision is non-existent or mission personnel are not being fully challenged by the situation.

Previous chapters have discussed subjects such as covenants, stages, conferences and related potential problems. This chapter presents a number of specific supervision problems. Some problems arise because of problem systems, while others grow out of special situations or human issues.

SYSTEMIC PROBLEMS

Shared Supervision

Mission personnel face the reality of working with shared supervision because multiple agencies are usually involved in their support and each agency shares in the supervision. In the past, management determined that only one person could be supervisor of an employee and that supervisor, in turn, was accountable.   In the past two decades this autocratic view of leadership in management has changed with the development of participatory or democratic management.   This management style includes people at all levels in evaluation and decision making; even supervisees participate in decisions.

Shared supervision among most mission personnel is a quasi--participatory management style, not full participatory management.   Each agency has its own public or constituency to whom it is responsible, so each agency has to maintain a degree of accountability and authority.

Mission personnel supervision should be divided among the agencies and supervisors so each knows the most productive way to help and stay within the limitations of their roles.   This is consistent with my definition of supervision as a support system.   Supervision is not a "Lone-Ranger" undertaking but the development of a mission personnel support system.

Shared supervision has built-in problems.   For one thing, it opens the gate to game playing.   Mission personnel may play the game "supervisory split."   Persons involved in the supervisory task may fail to recognize or adhere to division in the supervisory role. Their actions may undercut the role of the direct, local supervisor.

The covenant should be clear between all involved parties and organizations.   When a supervisor begins to violate the covenant, one or more of the other supervisors need to call for a clarification.   As circumstances arise, some areas may not be as clear, creating the need to renegotiate the covenant.   If mission personnel play "supervisory split," the other supervisors involved should be alerted.

Role Problems

Supervisors and mission personnel may suffer role problems. Friends may become supervisor and supervisee.   A budget committee member in a Baptist association may be the supervisee of the director of missions who is directly affected by the budget.   State missions directors, who turn over the supervision to the directors of missions, may have problems in releasing their role as the direct supervisor of the mission personnel. Mission agencies may create new problems of supervision so mission personnel formerly without close supervision become a part of a system which requires it.

Supervisors face role problems. A person who has never been a supervisor may be appointed to supervise mission personnel. He or she may be tempted to flaunt the role as supervisor, ignore it or develop a "buddy-buddy" relationship with the mission personnel. Role problems may not all be vocational. Young mission personnel moving out of seminary may face change from full-time student to full-time minister. This transition can cause an intense emotional shock. A role change may occur as a minister leaves a congregation and moves into a mission setting without the support system of a local congregation.

A serious danger in that latter kind of move is the wife's new role. In one setting, she was the queen bee of the congregation and a ministry partner with her husband. In an institutional setting, she probably has no role closely identified with her husband's role.

Mismatch

Mismatches do occur. Yet the idea of a mismatch may have been overplayed. In many cases where the differences between supervisor and supervisee seemed to point to a mismatch, fine supervisory relationships have developed. However, the supervisor and mission personnel should examine problems creating a mismatch: differences in age, race, socioeconomic background, experience, goals, and geographic origin. Rather than creating problems, differences have the potential of enriching the lives of both supervisor and supervisee.

Great differences are bound to limit the supervisory relationship: for example, when an Anglo supervises a Black, Indian, or Asian. Each has grown up in a different community. Each has unique needs. The supervisor will be limited; yet the relationship can be mutually satisfactory, with the covenant drawn in such a way as to meet realistically the expectations of the individuals and the system.

The covenant should hold each person accountable. The covenant and mutual expectations cut down the possibility of game playing where one or the other says, "But you don't understand how it is in my situation." The covenant yokes the supervisor and mission personnel together.

PERSONAL PROBLEMS

Change and Loss

Change may involve loss, even if change is for the better. The pastor who leaves a small congregation to pastor a congregation three times larger may soon wish to return to his former congregation. The pastor may miss the close circle of friends and the familiar power structure. Although it seems change was for the good, the individual may suffer a sense of loss. This is also true of a change of system such as moving from non-supervision to supervision.

Where loss occurs, anger follows. The anger may be internalized and denied or expressed and justified, but anger is a sign of the loss. Anger can be seen in such signs as withdrawal, pouting, emotional explosions or constant resistance. Whenever there is a change in supervision, the supervisor can expect anger. He should be prepared to deal with it in order to proceed with the supervisory task.

Resistance

Supervisors meeting resistance fight an uphill battle. They may feel as though they are pushing a car uphill by themselves. Resistance is no great mystery and can be unraveled. Supervisors need to tell the mission personnel that they perceive resistance and work with them to check the source. This is the honest way to handle resistance. Supervisors cannot help by closing their eyes to supervision or becoming legalistic and making demands regardless of resistance. The most helpful thing is to flush out the resistance where both can see it and deal with it.

Individualism

Mission personnel who have chosen a ministry on some frontier — racial, social, language or church starting — tend to be highly individualistic. While we applaud their individualism and independence, these characteristics can also hinder supervision. The supervision should help mission personnel recognize how the attributes of individualism or independence help and, conversely, when they do not.

Authority

Authority surfaces as an important part of a supervisory relationship. Supervisors may be afraid to assert authority and confront the mission personnel — or authority may be abused and demanding. Mission personnel may believe they are accountable to no one but God. Lines of authority should be drawn in the covenant between mission board and institution. Authority should be determined between supervisor and mission personnel. Their relationship should fall within the guidelines of the two covenants.

Responsibility

Each agency and person in the supervisory relationship must accept responsibility. Mission personnel may want the supervisor to assume their responsibility or rescue them. There may be trouble if the supervisor assumes more responsibility than called for in the covenant.

A good covenant includes the limits of responsibility of each agency and person. The supervisor needs to maintain accountability of the mission personnel. Supervisors also need to be supportive. Supervisors should note clues which show that the mission personnel are having problems dealing with their responsibility. Those who rely on religious cliches or phrases such as "the Lord's will," "praise God" and "the devil made me do it," may be avoiding responsibility. While theology includes the will of God, praise and demonic temptation, these may be used as escape mechanisms. They may avoid taking the responsibility for the good things because, if they did, they would have to bear the responsibility for the problems.

Inexperience

Sometimes supervisors may work with inexperienced people. Supervisees may have had experience in other areas but not in their new assignment. If overwhelmed, they may react with hyperactivity or inactivity. The supervisor should be prepared to provide "high" structure for inexperienced mission personnel. This requires more thorough reporting, more intense supervision. Yet the supervisor should not be occupied with trying to rescue the inexperienced mission personnel from making mistakes. All of us learn from our mistakes. However, the supervisor should be alert so that inexperienced mission personnel do not get into a grave situation.

When supervisors hold inexperienced mission personnel to a higher structure, they may face resistance. Supervisors can reduce friction by outlining the stages of supervision and explaining how the mission personnel will increasingly take charge of their own fates.

Identity

All persons face identity problems. Identity issues are especially difficult for young mission personnel. They are not only taking on a new role — moving from student to minister — but are also struggling with the move from adolescence to adulthood. They tend to think that at a magic age they will have it all together (as they perceive their seminary professors and supervisors do). They fail to realize everyone struggles to "put it together."

In dealing with young mission personnel, supervisors can provide a model by sharing their own continuing identity struggle. This takes insight, honesty and courage. The normal assumption is that mission personnel are going through identity stages in a healthy way. In spite of advanced years, some people continue to struggle to be free of their adolescence. These people may need therapy rather than supervision.

Theology

Occasionally, a supervisor faces the problem of supervising personnel with inadequate or defective theology. The theology of some may be excellent but merely not consistent with that of their constituency. Theology is personal — a matter worked out between the individual and God. However, a serious disparity in theologies between mission personnel and constituency causes conflict. The covenant relationship between the supervisor and mission personnel does not give the supervisor license to call mission personnel heretics or vice versa. Yet, supervisors need to help mission personnel realize this disparity is counter-productive to ministry.

And the supervisor should investigate beyond theological issues. For example, a supervisor asked about a recent seminary graduate under his supervision who did not believe in the virgin birth and who was ministering in a conservative congregation. While not minimizing the doctrinal issue, it seemed more was at stake than an intellectual doctrine. Perhaps the young man was rebellious and the rebellion was also showing up in other areas. The supervisor acknowledged this.

Verbalizing disbelief in the doctrine of the virgin birth may have caused problems in this setting; his rebellion could have reaped other kinds of trouble. If the supervisor dealt only with the doctrinal issue, he neglected a basic problem.

Supervisors should check sudden changes in theological stance of mission personnel. Many change under emotional pressures rather than through intellectual pursuit. The supervisor needs to understand reasons for sudden theological change. A person who suddenly becomes charismatic may be responding to a life stress rather than to an intellectual discovery.

Inadequate Preparation

Mission personnel may be prepared for other areas of ministry, but not for the task at hand. The supervisor needs to help mission personnel seek training or other preparation. As a support system, the supervisor needs resources to help with such problems.

Supervisors complain that seminaries inadequately prepare people for mission work. First, seminaries are often so large they cannot give individualized attention to students to determine their acquired skills. A second problem involves the learning readiness. Most persons learn best when actually faced with the situation. How many persons enter a building and immediately look for the fire exit but, if a fire suddenly breaks out, they quickly try to "learn." Until they face ministry situations, it is difficult for students to be real learners. Seminaries help students develop learning readiness for ministry when students participate in a good seminary supervision program. Continuing education is important for ministers as they return, with their experiences and needs, to the learning situation.

Passive-aggressive Behavior

Often supervisors have problems with passive-aggressive mission personnel. While quietly acquiescing to the supervisor's wishes for a while, the passive-aggressive person may blow up or in some other way try to sabotage the supervisory relationship. This type person often has difficulty taking initiative. The supervisor needs to note when mission personnel acquiesce to their suggestions but do not carry them out or fail to act on them enthusiastically. Supervisors need not examine the task perhaps as much as what is occurring in the supervisory relationship.

Work Habits

Nothing takes the place of work. Good planning not carried out is less effective than poor plans enthusiastically executed. Supervisors need to check mission personnel work level. The supervisor should be careful not to impose personal patterns of work. For example, mission personnel may work more intensively but for shorter periods of time than the supervisor. A workaholic supervisor should not impose his neurosis upon the mission personnel.

Family

Family problems which surface may be serious and capable of destroying the mission personnel's effectiveness. Erosion of the home in American society influences the minister's home. The mission personnel's family problems can easily arise with the amount of time demanded at work. Inadequate finances may also cause problems.

Finances

Finances may create a strain upon mission personnel who may face great economic pressures compared to people in other professions. Mature mission personnel may be financing their children's college educations. Others may be facing retirement with less than adequate retirement resources. Supervisors need to be sensitive to the fact that tension connected with inadequate finances may affect the functioning of mission personnel.

If there were no problems, there would be no ministers. If mission personnel had no problems, there would be no supervisors. The above list is incomplete. Every supervisor and all mission personnel can add other problems to this list, but these are among the most common.

SITUATIONAL PROBLEMS

Supervising at a Distance

Geographical distance between the supervisor and mission personnel can interfere with the supervisory task.   In these situations, supervisors may be tempted to play the game "wooden leg" and say, "If I were only closer I could do a good job of supervising." Supervision (i.e. support) may be especially needed where geographical distances are great.

No one denies that geographical distances fail to enhance supervision, but good planning can insure good supervision. The mail and the telephone can be used. Supervisory sessions may be planned to coincide with denominational meetings attended by both. Supervisors can plan to make longer visits with mission personnel, perhaps an overnight stay. There is no substitute for full cooperation between supervisor and mission personnel.

The covenant is very important when supervising at a distance. A clear and complete covenant gives the supervisee a "supervisor" at hand inasmuch as he or she can regularly review the covenant. This is a situation where a covenant may need to outline monthly goals and activities. The supervisor may have to lead in renegotiating the covenant every few months under these circumstances.

Supervising Older People

Sensitive supervisors, working with older supervisees, monitor health and energy concerns. Often the supervisor can spot a potential health problem more quickly than anyone else. Older persons have family concerns as well as younger persons. The family situation is different because the issue may be a child with marital difficulty or a health situation.

Many older persons have a wealth of wisdom available for the supervisor. I recall a deacon who had a masters degree in agriculture and who taught agriculture at the local high school. He asked his elderly father (who had less than an eighth grade education) to advise him about a crop he was raising. Age often gives a person perspective as well as information. Older people are usually teachable. They often want more training in a new situation than the supervisor offers. Sometimes they only need assurance that their previous experience is applicable to the present situation.

Aging can create supervisory problems. The older person who wants to live in the past can obstruct new ventures of an institution. I recall an elderly deacon who ruined deacons' meetings with the long stories he told throughout each meeting. You may need to meet with the person privately and express your concern about the effect of the extended conversations. You will usually get a good response if you express appreciation for the supervisee and his or her stories and add the need you have to expedite meetings.

Supervising Friends

While you might not ever seek to supervise a friend, there have been supervisors who found themselves having to do so. There may be role, authority and feeling problems in this situation. The alert supervisor will talk with the friend and define their respective roles and when the roles apply. There needs to be clear signals about when the person is in the role of supervisor and when they can relax in the role of friends. Probably no person more than the supervisor realizes that the supervisory authority is not because of his or her inherent superiority; it is a responsibility that comes with the position. It is wise for the supervisor to indicate that to the friend.

Friends often feel a sense of betrayal when a supervisor-friend agrees with another supervisee rather than with him or her. When the supervisor discusses the supervisory role with the friend at the beginning of the new supervisory relationship, the supervisor should clarify the possibility of this happening. However, assure the friend that this does not mean he or she is being rejected.

The covenant can help avoid problems where a person has to supervise a friend. Supervision can be contained within the framework of the covenant, while "normal" relationships remain outside the scope of the covenant. These factors should also be communicated to any other supervisees since they will know of the friendship and worry that they will be left out.

Supervising Unhealthy People

Perhaps the single most devastating thing that can happen in supervision is to have a supervisee who is emotionally unhealthy. It will interfere with his or her work and relationships. Unfortunately, it will also interfere with the supervisor's work and relationships. The supervisor has to spend an inordinate amount of time with the unhealthy supervisee, cleaning up his or her messes. The unhealthy person may gain a following so that the supervisor faces mutiny.

When you suspect a problem like this, determine the extent of the problem. Don't become vulnerable by keeping the problem to yourself. Ask the opinion of people who are knowledgeable and who can keep confidences. Enlist their support. They may need to help you get a person like this into therapy. The person may need some "mothering" which someone can provide. You may need protection from the workers' accusations or behavior which only someone else can give you.

You may have to bite the bullet and sever the supervisory relationship. Dismissing a person from a position is not easy for most people and, in American society, is filled with legal ramifications. The structure needs to be in place to meet these situations before they occur. Remember—it is easier to hire than to fire. Taking more time on the front end may mean less heartache later.

Supervising Cross Gender

The guiding principle of cross-gender supervision is respecting the other person and his or her feelings. What is innocent to the supervisor may be fearful to the supervisee. Any action or language which the supervisee interprets as demeaning will hinder the supervisory relationship. Avoid sex role stereotypes. Appraise the gifts of the individual.

Cross-gender supervision happens within a context. The community and the institution have a history and perceptions that help shape sex roles. Whether the supervisor and supervisee agree with these, they cannot ignore them. They need to address this issue before they begin the supervisory relationship.

Missionaries in foreign countries face cultural limitations about cross-gender supervision. A missionary couple employed a national husband and wife to help them with domestic tasks. The missionaries had difficulties until they learned that the national would only take orders from the man. Also any communication about work which the national woman needed to do had to be given to the husband to communicate to his wife.

Cross-gender supervision always raises the fear of sexual misconduct. Even the appearance of inappropriate behavior can be devastating. Several disciplines help deal with this. Practice an open-door policy whenever or wherever you hold a conference. Make notes about each conference including the time of beginning and ending and the subjects discussed.

Supervising Underqualified

Any competent person is underqualified at something. You may believe that your supervisee is underqualified. First of all, make sure the problem is being underqualified. You may not be aware of all the factors which are keeping the person from fulfilling your expectations. The person may be competent but untrained in the area where you need help. A simple training program might pay big dividends. If you find the person is underqualified, you may re-covenant with the person so he or she can function in an area where adequate. You will be wise to take care in initial interviews to determine the potential supervisee's qualifications. It is much easier to turn someone down initially than to terminate a person later.

Supervising Overqualified

An overqualified supervisee can be as big a problem as one who is underqualified. An overqualified supervisee can intimidate people, including the supervisor. The overqualified person can become bored and feel unappreciated since his or her skills are not fully utilized. You may need to move the overqualified person to a new situation that will provide more challenge. Sometimes this means going outside the primary employing institution to find the challenge.

Supervising in an Inadequate System

Some systems provide adequate structure for good supervision while others do not. You may be able to change the system to provide the structure, but that may take a long time, even if it were possible. You may be able to build the kind of structure you need with the covenant even if the system does not provide adequate structure. You will want to be honest with the supervisee before beginning the relationship. It is better that the supervisee enter the relationship aware that adjustments will have to be made to provide good supervision.

Supervising in a Task-oriented System

Many systems are task-oriented. Even religious systems have followed the traditional, task-oriented, corporate model. The covenant provides an opportunity to insert personhood issues into the supervision program. The supervisor can insist on the supervisee writing personhood goals into the covenant. During supervisory conferences, the supervisor can help the supervisee become sensitive to personhood issues.

Supervising in a Person-oriented System

A few systems become so person oriented that they overlook tasks that need to be done. These systems are preoccupied with individual hurts, injustices, theories and feelings. In these systems people need covenants with quantifiable goals and review times so they are held accountable to the goals.

CHAPTER 11

FINDING YOUR WAY
OUT OF SUPERVISORY TRAPS

Supervisors face traps that keep them from their supervisory responsibility or hinder their effectiveness. The sincere supervisor may be surprised by one of the traps. It is easy to despair and believe that dealing with the traps is what a supervisor does. Common supervisory traps are communication, time, confrontation/conflict, motivation and delegation. Since these traps are prominent in supervision, this chapter addresses these potential problems.

COMMUNICATION

My daughter came home from second grade one day crying and angry. When my wife asked her what was wrong, my daughter told her mother that her teacher had called her best friend a horse just because her friend had a cold. Her mother patiently explained the difference between "horse" and "hoarse." Communication is a difficult enterprise.

Problems in Communication

Supervisors and mission personnel can expect communication problems. Communication is mysterious enough when both parties try to make communication work. Greater problems arise in supervision where there is inadequate structure, resistance or unclear goals. Problems are compounded when supervision is cross-cultural.

Listening. Listening is a major problem in communication. Public schools spend millions of dollars teaching remedial as well as regular courses in reading. We spend more hours a day listening than reading, but who has ever taken a course on listening?

Good listening improves communication. One should actively listen rather than only sit in the geographical locale of the speaker. Ask, "Am I spending as much energy and concentrating as much when I listen as when I speak?" The supervisor who does not listen to mission personnel with concentration can expect to be heard with the same indifference. One of the best ways a supervisor can teach communication is by modeling listening. Supervisors who listen communicate caring and that they think the supervisee is important. Good listening is not only hearing words but receiving feeling behind those words. Words do not always bear the message; feeling behind the words may be a cry for help. Good listening is accomplished with the ears of the mind and the ears of the heart.

Context. Everyone communicates within a context. The context includes family and cultural background, goals, education and existing pressures. A supervisor within five years of retirement works from a different context than the twenty-five-year-old person in the first ministry position who dreams about the future job possibilities. The Anglo comes from an entirely different context than an Hispanic. Words may not mean the same to supervisor and mission personnel. Each reacts differently to ideas.

Regional idioms may also cause misunderstanding. Wendell Belew, former division director of the Home Mission Board, tells about sending a seminary student from Mississippi to preach in the hills of Kentucky. He instructed the student to stop at a certain place, pick up an elderly woman and take her to church. Later that week, when Belew asked the woman how she liked the young man, he was surprised to find out that she had been offended. The young man had offered to "carry her" to church. The Mississippi idiom of "carrying" people resulted in a gross communication problem.

Authority. Authority can create or alleviate communication problems. Observing an associate pastor lead a seminar, I noticed no one responded when he asked for feedback. After an hour, the pastor affirmed what he had heard from the associate and from that point there was stimulating dialogue. Titles, over-under relationships, personal charisma and forced relationships create communication problems. The supervisor should anticipate communication difficulties with mission personnel when a mission board assigns the supervisory role. The difficulties are not insurmountable but they do need to be addressed early in the supervisory relationship.

Supervisors can offer special opportunities for mission personnel to relate both their ideas and feelings about the supervisory roles, the ground rules and relationships. Supervisors should also promise to hear and seriously consider mission personnel when they communicate. Supervisors also need to clarify boundaries due to system requirements.

Setting. The setting influences communication. If the session occurs in the supervisor's office, the supervisor's role and authority is heightened because they are on the supervisor's turf. The desk behind which the supervisor sits communicates that something is between them. Free-flowing communication occurs in a neutral place or, at least one not closely identified with the supervisor. They should sit facing one another with no barriers in between. A man who is a sought-after expert in his field told of a job interview during which the dean sat behind his desk the whole time. The man perceived the dean as arrogant and impersonal. Consequently, he turned down the job offer.

Supervisors can examine their communication with supervisees. They can monitor whether they are communicating as a parent, a peer, a professor or in some other role. They may even become conscious of when they change communication styles.

The critical part of communication. The model on page 124 shows the options, factors and problems in the path of communication between two people. [1]

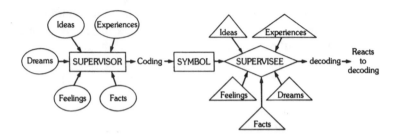

Both supervisor and supervisee operate in each situation with their own ideas, facts, experiences, feelings and dreams. Although the model has been drawn with all elements of equal importance, in reality the elements may be more like the following model. [2]

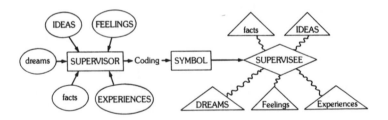

Communication appears impossible or at least miraculous. The supervisor codes communication and creates a symbol which is passed on to the mission personnel. Because of the variant frames of reference, no symbol is the perfect bearer of communication and a symbol may be counter-productive. At the same time, the symbol may be a way of refusing to disclose information. The phrase, "he hid his feelings," may also apply

[1]From *The Supervision of Mission Personnel* by Doran C. McCarty (Atlanta: Home Mission Board, SBC, 1983), p. 140.

[2]Ibid., p. 141.

to language which may prevent communication as well as permit it. With all of these possibilities of noncommunication or miscommunication, the supervisor and mission personnel need to double-check what is said in order to ensure communication. The model below shows this graphically. [3]

Theoretically this process could continue indefinitely until the

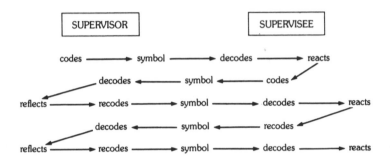

symbol means the same for both. However, at a certain point enough testing has occurred for people to realize they are communicating adequately or will never be able to communicate. Misunderstanding can be minimized by patiently testing the communication process.

Body language. Body language refers to bodily reactions or mannerisms. Everyone interprets body language whether or not they are conscious of it. We have heard people say, "I knew he wasn't telling me the truth because he couldn't look me in the eye." People communicate by what they do with their bodies as well as by their words. They communicate with the way they look at us, whether they cross their arms or legs, whether they lean toward or away from us, and by where they sit in relation to us. Usually people are unconscious of their body language.

Following a supervision training conference, I apologized for a colleague whose inappropriate remarks demonstrated that he

---

[3]Ibid.

did not understand what was being said. The leader said to me, "Yes, I noticed you cleared your throat every time he started to speak." The leader had picked up my unconscious body language. I could have offered some excuse about sinus drainage, but the truth was the leader had picked up my response when this particular person spoke.

In a non-threatening supervisory relationship, supervisors can interrupt conversations to discuss the meaning of any observed body language. This might sensitize the supervisor and mission personnel to intense feelings or resistance.

Formal and informal communication. Behind-the-scenes diplomatic negotiations often further international understandings more than the formal statements made by diplomats. Formal statements may be made to save face and hold traditional positions. Behind the scenes, diplomats may deal with issues in a realistic way. Supervisors and mission personnel will find these same conditions in formal and informal communication. Informal communication may help solve problems in ways that formal supervisory sessions cannot. Informal luncheon discussions may solve more problems than formal supervisory sessions. It is not the meal which makes a session informal, but the consciousness that they are no longer in a formal setting.

Structured communication. You structure communication by structuring the format. Oral communication is faster and allows for observation of body language. It is more spontaneous, less precise and it may open opportunities for game playing. If communication problems arise with oral data, supervisors should request written data.

Supervisors and mission personnel can structure "checking out" communication. The supervisor may need to ask the mission personnel, "What did you understand me to say?" Mission personnel may answer, "I understood you to say . . ." Feedback provides opportunity to check if what was said was appropriately communicated. Mission personnel should not say to the supervisor, "What you said was" but, "This is what I heard you say." Communication is the vehicle for supervision. When the vehicle is faulty, adequate supervision cannot occur.

Supervision may even be harmful rather than helpful without adequate communication.

TIME MANAGEMENT

The supervisor faces two time management problems—his or her own time management and the supervisee's time management. Time is our most important resource. You can't restore, replace or replenish it. Time will inevitably pass so we need to find how to make the most of it. Before agreeing to become a supervisor, a person should examine the time commitment which supervision will take. Supervision usually means that we have to make time adjustments. A new supervisory responsibility may be a good opportunity for a supervisor to do a time audit. This should be done occasionally anyway since we easily fall into non-productive time usage patterns.

When I ask seminar participants about their time problems, they often answer with the following list: interruptions, distinguishing between the urgent and important, setting priorities, planning, personal time, family time, self-discipline, phone delegation, saying yes instead of no and mail. However important these issues are, they are not as crucial as a person's perspective on time. In my opinion, time problems are not so much mechanical as personal.

Chronos and Kairos

Paul Tillich distinguished between the two Greek words for *chronos* and *kairos*. Chronos time denotes the sequence of events (the word "chronometer" come from chronos). This is clock time. Kairos means significant or meaningful time. Eric Rust called kairos "filled time." Kairos is time marked by meaningful events. Kairos is the way the Bible marked time. Isaiah referred to his experience in the temple as being ". . . in the year that King Uzziah died . . . ." People still mark time by significant events. They may refer to events as before or after we were married or had children. I recall one couple where the wife had been in a tragic accident that required multiple surgeries. Whenever they spoke of an event, they referred to it being either before or after the accident.

The Euro-American culture is very chronos conscious. How many adult Americans do you see who don't wear a watch? Nearly everyone does. German trains run on the minute. Television operates on the split-second. Once I mentioned to a missionary that I would meet him at 4:00 p.m. He asked, "Is that African or British time?" He said that where he served in Africa, a 4:00 p.m. appointment would mean that it would not start before 4:00 p.m.

Mechanics and Personhood

During the 1930's, a fad developed which consisted of efficiency experts doing time and motion studies. The efficiency expert used a stop watch to measure how much time each motion took and recommended alternative approaches. There are efficiency problems. We may write letters by hand (which our secretaries can't read) rather than use a dictating device.

The mechanics of time management and efficiency studies apply to chronos time. You can deal with these mechanics by calendars, reminders, deadlines and time-saving techniques. These are important and should be examined regularly for efficiency.

However, the real time problems usually come from personhood issues. We don't see the meaningfulness in what we do. We resent having to keep a schedule. We want to do what we want to do when we want to do it. We are compulsive rather than disciplined. We don't like to say "no." We do what we like to do instead of what needs doing. We may be fearful. We may avoid the new. We are afraid to delegate. We don't ask for help.

Ego Strength and Time Management

Time management is not so much the use of tricks to save time as having the strength of character to take charge of your life and manage your time. Personality inventories have a category called "ego strength." Shortly after I began using these inventories, I noticed the importance of ego strength. Ego strength refers to how well we think of ourselves. If our ego strength is low, we don't think well enough of ourselves to take charge of our lives so we let others manage us. A person with a low ego strength has difficulty saying "no."

The ability to say no is most important in managing time. If we cannot say "no," others set our agenda. We keep getting loaded with tasks others don't want and as a result we don't have time for our own life agenda. In a T.V. commercial a man says, "I can do that," "I can do that," "I can do that." Then he turns and says, "How can I do that?" Taking the airline that sponsored the commercial will not solve your problem of not being able to say "no."

Ego strength is one of the personhood issues in time management. There are some mechanical things you can do when you have these problems, but they do not deal with the root cause.

Meaningful Time

What is meaningful to you? You deserve meaning in your life. Part of planning is to provide time for your events or achievements. This is kairos time. Use the following format to make a list of the twenty most meaningful events in your life.

	A	B	Event
1.	___	___	_____
2.	___	___	_____
3.	___	___	_____
4.	___	___	_____
5.	___	___	_____
6.	___	___	_____
7.	___	___	_____

8. ____ ____ _____

9. ____ ____ _____

10. ____ ____ _____

11. ____ ____ _____

12. ____ ____ _____

13. ____ ____ _____

14. ____ ____ _____

15. ____ ____ _____

16. ____ ____ _____

17. ____ ____ _____

18. ____ ____ _____

19. ____ ____ _____

20. ____ ____ _____

In the column marked "A" write one of the symbols below to indicate the kind of meaningful event or achievement. Use only one symbol per event even if you think two would apply.

V = vocation
$ = financial
R = recreational
P = physical
S = social
F = family
E = educational
C = civic
* = spiritual

When you finish putting these symbols in column "A," place in column "B" your age when the event took place.

Now you are ready to make an analysis. See how many events were vocational, etc. See if an age pattern is evident in these events. Were most of these events recent or several years ago? This will give you some clues about your meaningful time. [4]

Maybe in heaven we will spend each moment doing what we like doing, but that isn't likely on earth. A friend, considering a job offer, said that he liked doing 60 percent of the job but not the other 40 percent. Every job has its down side. If we enjoy people, we may despise the paper work. However, without the paper work the system won't support us working with people. I may like the office work if people would leave me alone. I may like research but students get in the way. Everyone will have to pay for the privilege of doing meaningful things by taking care of the institution's agenda.

Taking Charge of Your Life and Job

God gave you your life and time as a stewardship. You can't forfeit these to anyone else and fulfill your stewardship. You need to be in charge. Even when you commit your life to a job or agency, you need to do it to fulfill your stewardship and do it as a conscious decision. It is easy to be blown off course by every person or crisis that comes along. Supervisors can let others determine their life and job. When the supervisor gets in charge of his or her life, this provides a model for the supervisee. Below are some things to consider in your time management.

1. Life goals. If you know where you are headed in life, you can use your time to prepare yourself. Without life goals you may experience confusion and depression. For example, what are your financial goals for retirement? If you have that goal in

---

[4]The preceding exercise is taken from *LifeAudit: A Planning Guide for Ministry and Personal Growth* by Doran C. McCarty (Nashville: Seminary Extension of the Southern Baptist Seminaries, 1991), pp. 9-24.

mind, you may save yourself anxiety and even years when you approach retirement. It will be too late to set that goal when you are 55 or 60.

2. Plan. An associational director of missions used to say to the pastors, "Plan your work and work your plan." You can plan best based on your life goals. Planning is both long term and short term. Good planning involves setting priorities. You can enhance even personal planning by consulting others.

3. Schedule. Planning leads to scheduling events on a calendar. A supervisor can help a supervisee by insisting that he or she schedule personal and family time in the same manner as vocational time. Share your schedule with your significant people so they won't try to plan your time for you.

4. Develop routine. One of the great time helps is routine. Many things can be done on a routine basis so that you don't have to spend time re-inventing the wheel. The routines should be examined regularly to see if they are the best.

5. Do your job. You need to do your job. A supervisor may discover he or she is doing someone else's job. A pastor becomes an associational director of missions and continues to do "pastor jobs." One person I know moved into a job where he had a secretary but kept doing his own typing. He got fired because his supervisor said he couldn't afford to pay him $40,000 a year as a department manager while he did the work of a $12,000-a-year secretary.

6. Multiple uses. It takes a large amount of time to prepare for many tasks. You should plan multiple uses for the material you prepare. You can use sermon and illustrative material again in different contexts. If your preparation is research on a book of the Bible, a technical subject, or a conference theme, you may want to find other places to deliver the material or use it in other addresses. I have turned down opportunities to do the annual Bible study for a church because I would not be able to do the Bible study several times and I could not justify the amount of preparation time required for only one presentation.

7. Keep a journal. When you keep a journal, you have the opportunity to examine your time usage. It will be more than minutes or hours spent on specific tasks. It will also give you a picture of whether you are doing the meaningful things. An effective supervisor will ask a supervisee to prepare a journal from time to time.

The Time Trap

Time is one of the traps of supervision. The supervisor as well as the supervisee can get trapped into bad time management. It is a trap because once you get caught, it takes so much time and energy to escape.

CONFRONTATION AND CONFLICT

There is a myth, based on no fact I know, that there is no confrontation where Christians operate. History, ancient and contemporary, dispute that myth. I usually find where there is no confrontation, there are mindless people. Instead of avoiding confrontation and conflict, we do better when we learn how to handle it in a Christian manner. There is confrontation in all human relationships and conflict in many. [5] It should not surprise us, then, that these appear in supervisory relationships.

Let me distinguish between confrontation and conflict. People often use these terms interchangeably but, if at all possible, we should distinguish between them.

Confrontation is to face, challenge, and encounter. Conflict is to be antagonistic, incompatible, contradictory, and irreconcilable.

Authors and speakers have made the term "conflict management" popular, but I believe this is an inappropriate term. You may be able to manage confrontation to some extent but not conflict. If you could manage conflict, you could manage avoiding it. I prefer to speak of handling conflict rather than managing it.

---

[5]This material on confrontation and conflict is an expansion of the ideas in *Working with People* by Doran C. McCarty (Nashville: Broadman Press, 1986), pp. 107-123.

Why Do We Confront?

We probably can not avoid confrontation all the time because of life situations. There are times when the results of confrontation are not worth the effort. You will remember the old saw that a dog can whip a skunk but it isn't worth the effort. A few people need constant confrontation to feed them emotionally. There are legitimate reasons and times for confrontation.

1. Care. David Augsburger has written a book, *Caring Enough to Confront*. In the book he created the term "carefronting." Unless we care, we will not confront. We may care for the well-being of the other person, our own welfare, the status quo, an organization, a possession, an idea or a dream. But we will not confront unless we care.

2. Clarify. When we need to clarify, we often have to confront. Another person has answers that we do not have. We can only guess at their feelings, dreams or plans. They have to tell us or we won't know. If they do not volunteer the information we need, we will have to ask (confront).

3. Change. Whether we want to change or guard the status quo against change, we will have to confront. At some point everything changes and without confrontation the particular changes may not be desirable.

4. Growth. People need to grow. Some need to be confronted in order to stimulate growth. If left unconfronted, they continue in their unproductive patterns. The same principle applies to organizations.

The slogan "no pain, no gain" applies to confrontation. Where there is confrontation, there is usually pain. Suffering shows the sensitivity.

Why Do We Avoid Confrontation?

Proverbs 27:5 says, "Better is open rebuke than hidden love." Having the truth of that passage, why do we avoid conflict? We can observe several reasons for this.

1. It's not nice (or it's not Christian). We carry emotional baggage from childhood marked with "it's not nice" tags. Mothers tell sons not to fight because "it's not nice." She separates quarreling siblings, usually sending them to different rooms so they cannot even communicate. Cultural baggage adds to the avoidance. Some cultures avoid confrontation (or the Euro-American form of confrontation) and other cultures make confrontation typical. I notice that my Italian friends have little difficulty with confrontation. They confront intensely and love no less.

Christians, with sentimental notions about religion, say "Christians don't do things like that!" This attitude risks equating meekness, kindness and gentleness with acquiescence. Jesus, as shown in the New Testament, did not avoid confrontation with either friends or foes. We may not confront to keep peace and harmony. Avoidance of confrontation does not create (nor conserve) peace and harmony but equates peace and harmony with passiveness.

2. Fear. We fear getting hurt or hurting someone else. People can get hurt especially when confrontation turns to conflict. Healthy people are not so fragile and can stand confrontation. Instead of falling to pieces, healthy people often gain strength from confrontation. Competitive people may fear losing. Avoidance spares their fragile egos.

3. Passivity. Some people had rather switch than fight. They think that appeasement will make problems go away. One interpreter calls them "abdicrats" since they would rather abdicate their "throne" than contend.

Confront to Negotiate

Negotiation is important in society. People have to negotiate treaties, contracts and purchases. The person skilled in confrontation has the advantage in negotiation. The skillful confronter knows whether to start confrontation or create conditions so others will have to begin. The skillful confronter may become anxious but will not be intimidated during negotiation. A minister went to a foreign country to work with the missionaries in the country. He carried some modest electronic equipment for mission work. While he would give the equipment to the missionary, he understood the possibility of having to pay duty tax on it. When the customs officer wanted to require a customs tax, the minister, practiced in the skill of confrontation, refused to let the customs officer intimidate him. He negotiated until the officer stamped the equipment as duty free.

Do not confront to punish. In a healthy person there is a reason for every. behavior even if it is not the best option. Confront to negotiate.

Whom to Confront

Confront healthy people who can change. Neurotics need care from therapists rather than confrontation from a supervisor. You will gain nothing by confronting a sick person. Sometimes we do not have an option when an unhealthy person creates conflict. Confront people who can make a difference. Each quiver has only so many arrows, so make them count. Good supervisors confront their supervisees. Someone has assigned the supervisee to the supervisor and that creates responsibility. When a supervisor confronts someone else in the system, it creates the possibility of a backlash since it is as if you were correcting someone else's child.

Qualities of a Good Confronter

1. Caring. Nothing takes the place of caring. Whenever we care, we have won a large part of any battle. If we don't care, we won't confront.

2. Insightful. Paul spoke of discernment in Philippians 1:9. People who do well at confrontation need this discernment. An insightful person can conceptualize a situation rather than become angry.

3. Courage. Insight is not enough. An effective confronter has courage to initiate action and withstand the wills of others.

4. Patience. Patience is not passiveness but keeping attention on an issue without aggressiveness. A person who confronts and retreats will not be effective. The competent confronter keeps pressure on others until they are open to negotiation. Change comes from thawing a situation, changing it and refreezing it so that it stays in place. If you thaw, change and do not have the patience for it to freeze, it will drop back to its original level.

Good Outcomes

Good can come from confrontation. People and organizations can change for the better. We can be too close to confrontive situations to recognize the value of the confrontation. You can reach goals. You may find unity through confrontation because you realize that you can live through it and live or work together. Confrontation also breeds creativity through the meeting of differing ideas.

Bad Outcomes

When confrontation reaches a level of conflict, bad things can happen. Military cemeteries, divorce and bankruptcy courts attest to this. You can lose your job and status. People do not always make up and live happily ever after. You may lose future opportunities.

How to Handle Conflict

Situations move from confrontation to conflict. When healthy people want to solve problems, they often can avoid conflict. Your use of confrontation may help avoid conflict. If you cannot avoid conflict, there are some things you can do that will help the situation.

1. Anticipate conflict. You are at a disadvantage when conflict surprises you. When you anticipate conflict, you can prepare for it. Anticipation helps avoid flashes of anger followed by damaging verbal abuse. Good anticipation allows a person to plan strategy rather than claim a position untimely.

2. Develop good attitudes. Develop good attitudes toward conflict as a way to prepare yourself. A person who becomes surly, belligerent, passive or acquiescent towards conflict has not prepared adequately for conflict. Positive results come when a person believes there is the possibility of a mutual solution. Western society is very competitive, but that competitiveness may get in the way during an attempt to handle conflict. People are made in God's image, so even those who engage in conflict with us deserve our respect. They have the same right as you to state their opinions.

Avoid dangers. You will face the temptation to surround yourself only with people who agree with you. That is comforting but counterproductive. It only insulates you for a short time and may allow the pressure you face to increase. One trap is to emphasize loyalty and cooperation and make disagreement sound like disloyalty and rebellion. If you pour oil on troubled waters rather than deal with the issue, the future storm will wash the oil away. You can gloss over differences, but it does not bring harmony. In fact people may feel "put down" if you do not take their opinions seriously. When you cut others down to strengthen your position, you set up an explosive situation. Listen to others rather than jump to conclusions. People need to be heard.

While ambiguity may buy time, later people will feel betrayed because they misread the ambiguous statement. Politicians use divide-and-conquer strategy, but it does not work with teams or in a fellowship. Depersonalize dissent rather than accuse.

Cautions. Condition yourself emotionally before conflict happens. You need to be both tough and tender during conflict. Do not cry "wolf." Eventually people desert leaders who constantly claim that others abuse them. Communicate real crises to people. You cannot handle conflict successfully alone. Be careful not to create more conflicts in settling a conflict. Improper resolution breeds more conflicts. Do not fight a battle over yourself. You can only lose the war. Let others conduct a battle that is over you.

2. Analyze. The powers to analyze are important. We teach people to read books, but effective leaders need to know how to read situations. This is critical in handling conflict.

The nature of conflict. Conflict may be personal or systemic. If personal, it may be a struggle within a person or between persons. Systemic conflict involves organizations, institutions or relationships. The nature of conflict is not always clear, and the apparent issue may only be a smokescreen. Sources of conflict may be reality, fantasy, fears and dreams. It may come from history or the present. The problem may be logistical, informational, status or a clash of values.

The depth of conflict. The more people care, the deeper the conflict. People may vote politely on a resolution about Bosnia but fight vehemently over dividing a Sunday School class. An issue that deals with the whole of life generates more feelings than conflict over a single issue. When an issue is a surface one, it may not create a threat if people treat one another with dignity. A complex issue that threatens principles or a way of life can become turbulent.

Dynamics of conflict. Conflicts differ. The person who controls systems is important since he or she can calm or excite conflict. In a large bureaucracy the system tends to control the system itself. People make investments and want to protect them. These are emotional as well as financial investments. This creates conflict when they believe someone threatens their investments. Decisions may be necessary in conflict. The nature and timing of these decisions are inherent in the dynamics.

One of the dynamics of conflict is the position of the persons involved with the conflict related to the leader. The farther the conflict is from the leader, the less critical the conflict. If the persons close to the leader defend him or her, the leader is relatively safe as long as the leader relies on these defenders. The chart on the next page displays how a pastor can view potential problems with persons relative to their position to the pastor. [6]

The term of the conflict. When conflict is long term, it grinds people down. If they know that the conflict is situational rather than chronic, they may be able to sustain their equilibrium. People have to deal with long-term conflict differently than short-term conflict.

Cost of the conflict. Conflict costs. The cost may be time, energy, self-esteem, money, relationships. Costs are real. Mar-

---

[6]From *Working with People* by Doran C. McCarty (Nashville: Broadman press, 1986), p. 116.

riages break up and churches split. As one analyzes conflict, he or she should determine if the conflict will be worth the costs.

Determine the conflict phase. Authors have described phases of conflicts. One list provides five phases: [7] (1) Anticipation, (2) Conscious but unexpressed differences, (3) Discussion, (4) Open dispute, (5) Open conflict.

---

[7] These phases come from material prepared by the Church Administration department of the Baptist Sunday School Board of the Southern Baptist Convention.

It is serious if you are unaware of the phase of conflict. You cannot turn back the clock to an earlier phase. Trying to deal with conflict in the wrong phase can be disastrous. When you close your eyes to the progress of conflict into new phases, you leave yourself at a disadvantage.

3. Consider alternatives. What are your alternatives? Make a list. How will I try to settle the conflict? Win-win? Win-lose? Lose-lose? What approach will I take? Passive? Aggressive? Passive-aggressive? Assertive? Do I have to have a life and death struggle now, or can I live to fight another day perhaps with advantages I do not have now?

4. Decide. Effective leaders will have to make decisions during conflict. Timely decisions help settle conflicts in early stages. The leader has to make decisions rather than forfeit decision making. No decision is perfect, but decisions can be effective. Since decisions are not perfect, it is unwise to absolutize decisions. Bernard Baruch (in 1936) said that if you could guarantee that he would be right 51 percent of the time, he would make a million dollars a day on the stock market. The temptation to absolutize decisions puts things in black-white, right-wrong or perfect-useless categories when every decision is a mixed bag.

5. Implement decisions. No decision is more effective than its implementation. Conflict remains until there is good implementation. Decision without implementation opens the door for more conflict.

6. Care for people's needs. People in conflict need care. They have crises that need attention. The wise leader takes care of people's hurts regardless of where they are in the conflict. All people deserve respect. When you are disrespectful, you even alienate your supporters.

Supervisors want to get jobs done without confrontation and conflict. Often confrontation is a good way to define the job and problems. Confrontation may short circuit conflict. Good confrontation is an effective tool for doing supervision.

MOTIVATION

The motivation trap is double-edged. Some supervisors avoid conscious efforts to motivate. They feel no need of external motivation and assume "sincere" workers need none. However, other supervisors feel the need to provide intense motivation. People do not work without motivation. The motivation can come from within or externally. It can be appropriate or inappropriate. We can avoid the motivation trap by being motivated ourselves, providing information and relying on appropriate motivators.

Few people in religious work are motivated by money. A handful of Elmer Gantrys should not determine our estimate of motivation. Most people doing religious work are motivated by belief systems and human need.

A major motivational force is for the leader to be motivated. If the leader is energetic and enthusiastic, this often affects others. Few people are more enthusiastic than the leader. The leader who works hard can expect those around him or her to be motivated. If the leader is passive, he or she will not generate energy among colleagues.

People are motivated by different things because they themselves are different. Personality inventories point to differences among people. What turns on one person doesn't turn on another. Ideas motivate some people, while programs, things or people motivate others. Needs motivate people. Abraham Maslow related motivation to a hierarchy of needs. [8] Maslow identified five human needs: physiological, security, social, ego and self-fulfillment. He said that the lower order needs (physiological and security) have to be met before the higher order needs are relevant.

R. Lofton Hudson, a pastor, counselor and author, in a conversation with me, suggested four motivators: guilt, shame, reality and love. Since that conversation I have added three others; anger, greed and dreams.

---

[8]Abraham Maslow, *Motivation and Personality* (New York: Harper & Row, 1954).

Guilt is a powerful force in normal people. It is the feeling that we are responsible for wrong and that we are to blame. We have the inherent need to "even the score." This is how people use guilt as a motivator. They provide a way to "even the score." A major catalyst in the Protestant Reformation was Tetzel (and others) selling indulgences for sin which was an institutional way of evening the score. Some people need help resolving their guilt feelings, but when a person manipulates the guilt feelings of others for his or her own purposes, it is wrong. It is also self-defeating. If people resolve their guilt feelings, they are no longer motivated by the guilt. However, if they do not resolve the guilt feelings, they can suffer depression, erosion of self-esteem or even commit suicide.

People confuse shame with guilt. Shame refers to dishonor and humiliation without wrongdoing. Shame uses "what if" rather than reality. Those who use shame tend to be game players.

Hudson said that some people (especially sociopaths) have little or no sense of guilt or shame. They can only be motivated by reality or fear. Fear can be a proper motivation where there is real danger. People who would not respond to ideals may respond to reality and fear. Supervisors who use fear are vulnerable to supervisees believing that they are crying wolf. Supervisors should provide facts and let supervisees decide on the reality of the situation. Of course, there are emergencies where supervisors must take direct action. Also supervisors may have to be more direct where supervisees are functioning in a different context than normal.

Love is a great motivator. People make enormous sacrifices for love. Love of God and country has motivated people to martyrdom and heroism. Love is an improper motivator when the object of love is wrong. A supervisor should not ask people to act out of friendship for the supervisor but from their love for God.

Anger motivates. Coaches post news releases on bulletin boards to anger and motivate players before a big game. Anger is a dangerous motivator. As an emotion, anger is not stable. Another emotion (self-preservation, pity, etc.) may replace it. Anger may be redirected toward the wrong person (including the supervisor). Anger may grow and get out of hand. Peacemaking and motivating by anger are poor bedfellows.

Paul declared that "the love of money is the root of all evil." [9] Is this what we call greed? Greed motivates many (if not all) people. It creates great energy levels. Greed is the dark side of ambition. A supervisor may want to motivate a person to achieve, but this can misfire and stimulate greed.

Dreams motivate. When a group shares a dream, they motivate one another. Bob Dale wrote a book, *To Dream Again*, that is a testimony to the power of dreams. Churches dream of new buildings and ministries and make enormous sacrifices to fulfill the dreams. A staff that dreams together works together.

Give people attention. People respond to attention. Elton Mayo of the Harvard Graduate School of Business Administration and his team performed experiments on motivation at the Western Electric plant in Hawthorne, Illinois. They experimented with several actions that stimulated productivity, but after some time their work level returned to normal. The researchers found that the secret was the attention given to the employees, not the specific action.

One motivation trap is failing to motivate people or doing it improperly. The supervisor invests time wisely when he or she spends time motivating.

DELEGATION

Delegation is a good way to expand ministry. Successful supervision and time management depend on good delegation. Where there is no delegation, there is no reason for a staff or volunteers. It should be real delegation, not "rubber band" delegation where everything has to come back to the "delegator." Delegation must not be easy since so many people have trouble with it.

---

[9] 1 Timothy 6:10.

Leaders' Problems in Delegating

Leaders have trouble delegating because of perfectionism. What perfectionists do is exemplary. How can they trust anyone else to be so perfect? Even when someone does a good job, it may not satisfy the perfectionist. A non-perfectionist may realize that he or she can do the work better than the supervisee. How is a supervisee going to gain skill without the opportunities to do the tasks? The supervisor may be afraid that the person can do the job better than he or she. While this may be a blow to the ego, a good supervisor will try to make this happen. If a supervisor chooses good people, they will surpass the supervisor in the job.

The supervisor may fear losing control through delegation. Despite protests, the supervisor may enjoy being "harried" because that is a way to get sympathy and feel needed (maybe indispensable). Some people are good at a job, but they do not know how to instruct others to do the job. Their skills at the job may be better than their teaching skills. The supervisor may not have the patience to stay at the mentoring task. The good delegator can help another understand the job conceptually and function well in the job. One thing that can complicate delegation is that the supervisor may enjoy doing the task and have difficulty letting go.

The Process for Good Delegation

There are several steps involved in good delegation.

1. Define goals. You won't be able to delegate well if you can't define the goals. It is important to agree on the goal, the task and how it will be measured.

2. Authority. Good delegation is not possible unless the supervisee has the authority to do the job. Delegation without authority only leads to frustration.

3. Communicate. You need to communicate the responsibility and authority to the supervisee and the rest of the staff. If a church is involved, you need to communicate to the congregation.

4. Train. Any supervisee should have the advantage of

training. This may be extensive for someone who has not worked in the special area of responsibility, but it may be minimal for mature and experienced persons.

5. Initiate. You and the supervisee will have a greater comfort level if you are on hand at the beginning to help him or her get started. When you are familiar with the situation, you may not be sensitive to what it means to do something for the first time.

6. Monitor. Establish a monitoring process at the beginning. You should not surprise the supervisee after the project starts.

7. Provide. Each task has needs. It may be chalk for the instructor, crayons for the children, sheet rock for the builders.

8. Evaluate. Set up a time and process for evaluation when you begin the delegation. Everyone deserves feedback.

Delegation is one of the essential ingredients of effective supervision. You are trying to extend your ministry through supervision and this implies delegation. It is disappointing to have everything else ready and fall into a trap that keeps you from doing good delegation.

BIBLIOGRAPHY

Audiovisuals

Mattone, John. *Street Smart Supervision.* Six audiocassettes published by Mattone Enterprises, Forestdale, Massachusetts, 1989.

Books

Blanchette, Melvin C., John Compton, and Barry Estadt. *The Art of Clinical Supervision.* New York: Paulist Press, 1987.

Cecil, Earl A., William J. Engel, and Earl F. Lundgren. *Supervision.* Columbus, Ohio: Grid, Inc., 1978.

Coll, Regina. *Supervision of Ministry Students.* Collegeville, Minnesota: The Liturgical Press, 1992.

Dalox, Laurent A. *Effective Teaching and Mentoring.* San Francisco: Jossey-Bass Publishers, 1990.

Damon, Roberta. *Relationship Skills* in the "Leadership Skills for Women" series. Birmingham: Woman's Missionary Union, SBC, 1993.

Gillespie, Karen R. *Creative Supervision.* New York: Harcourt Brace Jovanovich, Inc., 1981.

Hamlin, Judy. *Group Building Skills* in the "Leadership Skills for Women" series. Birmingham: Woman's Missionary Union, SBC, 1994.

Harral, Harriet. *Communication Skills* in the "Leadership Skills for Women" series. Birmingham: Woman's Missionary Union, SBC, 1994.

Hunter, George I. *Supervision and Education—Formation for Ministry.* Cambridge, Massachusetts: Episcopal Divinity School, 1982.

Jones. C. David. *The Pastoral Mentor.* Richmond, Virginia: Skipworth Press, Inc., 1980.

Levin, Stanley, Noel T. Parisien, and Daniel Thursz. *Handbook on Volunteers in Army Community Service.* Alexandria, Virginia: Human Resources Research Organization, 1969.

Lloyd, Debbie. *Time Management Skills* in the "Leadership Skills for Women" series. Birmingham: Woman's Missionary Union, SBC, 1994.

McCarty, Doran C. *Developing Support Systems for Missionaries.* Developing Support Systems for Missionaries. Atlanta: Home Mission Board, SBC, 1991.

_____. *Handbook on Supervision.* Atlanta: Home Mission Board, SBC, 1991.

_____. *LifeAudit: A Planning Guide for Ministry and Personal Growth.* Nashville: Seminary Extension of the Southern Baptist Seminaries, 1991.

_____. *Supervising Ministry Students.* Atlanta: Home Mission Board, SBC, 1978.

_____. *The Supervision of Mission Personnel.* Atlanta: Home Mission Board, SBC, 1983.

_____. *Supervision for Volunteers.* Atlanta: Home Mission Board, SBC, 1979, 1981, 1982, 1989.

_____. *Working with People.* Nashville: Broadman Press, 1986.

McDonough, Reginald M. *Working with Volunteers in the Church.* Nashville: Broadman Press, 1976.

Melnico, William B. and Jan Mennig. *Elements of Police Supervision.* Beverly Hills, California: Glencoe Press, 1969.

Munson, Carlton E., editor. *Family of Origin Applications in Clinical Supervision.* New York: Haworth Press, 1984.

Murray, Margo. *Beyond the Myths and Magic of Mentoring: How to Facilitate an Effective Mentoring Program.* San Francisco: Jossey-Bass Publishers, 1991.

Nelson, William R. *Ministry Formation for Effective Leadership.* Nashville: Abingdon Press, 1988.

Pettes, Dorothy E. *Staff and Student Supervision: A Task-centered Approach.* Boston: George Allen and Unwin, 1979.

Pohly, Kenneth H. *Transforming the Rough Places: The Ministry of Supervision.* Dayton, Ohio: Whaleprints, 1993.

Schooley, Shirley. *Conflict Management Skills* in the "Leadership Skills for Women" series. Birmingham: Woman's Missionary Union, SBC, 1994.

Sellner, Edward C. *Mentoring: The Ministry of Spiritual Kinship.* Notre Dame, Indiana: Ave Maria Press, 1990.

Smith, Cameron C. *Guides for Supervisors.* Washington, D.C.: U.S. Department of Agriculture, 1969.

_____. *The Standard Manual for Supervisors.* Waterford, Connecticut: Bureau of Business Practice, 1977.

Steere, David A., editor. *The Supervision of Pastoral Care.* Louisville: Westminster/John Knox Press, 1989.

Thomas, J. W. *Bi/Polar: A Positive Way of Understanding People.* Richardson, Texas: Bi/Polar, Inc., 1978.

Torrance, E. Paul. *Mentor Relationships.* Buffalo, New York: Bearly Limited, 1984.

Van Dersal, William. *The Successful Supervisor: In Government and Business.* Third Edition. New York: Harper and Row, 1974.

Von der Embse, Thomas J. *Supervision: Managerial Skills for a New Era.* New York: MacMillan, 1987. Also see the companion Instructor's Resource Guide by the same title.

White, Ernest. *The Art of Human Relations.* Nashville: Broadman Press, 1985.

With a Servant Heart: Perspectives on Women in Leadership. Birmingham: Woman's Missionary Union, SBC, 1992.

INDEX